Rhythm in Drama

Rhythm in Drama

Kathleen George

University of Pittsburgh Press

Published by the University of Pittsburgh Press, Pittsburgh, Pa., 15260
Copyright © 1980, University of Pittsburgh Press
All rights reserved
Feffer and Simons, Inc., London
Manufactured in the United States of America

Library of Congress Cataloging in Publication Data

George, Kathleen, 1943–
 Rhythm in drama.

 Includes index.
  1. Drama—Technique.   2. Rhythm.   I. Title.
PN1693.G4   808.2   79-24432
ISBN 0-8229-3416-7
ISBN 0-8229-5316-1 pbk.

Excerpts from *A Delicate Balance* by Edward Albee, copyright © 1966 by Edward Albee, are reprinted by permission of Atheneum Publishers and Jonathan Cape Ltd. Excerpts from Samuel Beckett's *Waiting for Godot* © 1954 by Grove Press are reprinted by permission of Grove Press, Inc., and Faber & Faber Ltd., London. Excerpts from *Hay Fever* © copyright 1927 by Noel Coward, copyright renewed 1954, are reprinted by permission of the Estate of Noel Coward. Excerpts from *The Wild Duck, The Master Builder,* and *Hedda Gabler* are reprinted by permission of Airmont Publishing Co., Inc. Excerpts from *Ghosts,* translated by William Archer, are reprinted from *A Treasury of the Theatre.* ed. John Gassner, by permission of Charles Scribner's Sons. Excerpts from Sean O'Casey's *The Plough and the Stars* are reprinted by permission of Macmillan, London and Basingstoke. Excerpts from *A Slight Ache* © 1961 by Harold Pinter are reprinted by permission of Grove Press, Inc., and Eyre Methuen Ltd. Excerpts from *Arms and the Man* are reprinted by permission of The Society of Authors on behalf of the Bernard Shaw Estate. Excerpts from Strindberg's *The Father* are reprinted courtesy of Branden Press, Inc., 21 Station Street, Brookline Village, Boston, Mass., 02147.

In memory of my father

Contents

Preface

'Tis here. / 'Tis here. / 'Tis gone.
—*Hamlet*, 1.1.141–42

Rhythm often seems as puzzling and elusive to us as Hamlet's Ghost is to the sentinels of the guard. When we look for it, it does not show itself. When we talk about something else, it appears, only to move quickly away. Rhythm is, by its very nature, fascinating and powerful, but like the Ghost, it does not speak upon command. I have had to content myself with letting it appear to me when it would; and when it has, rather than command it to speak, and scare it away, I have simply followed it for as long as I could, for as long as its shape remained visible to me. I hope that my observations will be useful to other ghost followers.

The first chapter of this book is a sampling of artists, critics, and aestheticians who have tried to describe rhythm or who have concerned themselves with the rhythmic properties of drama. To many readers this material will be familiar ground. At any rate, it serves to remind us of the enormous scope of rhythm. Succeeding chapters contain observations on the ways rhythm, on the occasions when it reveals itself, tends to shape our emotions and perceptions.

Acknowledgments

My debts are many, but "brief let me be." I would like to thank the following friends and colleagues for their support: Attilio Favorini, Trevor Melia, Leon Katz, Andrew Welsh, Diane Ritchey, Suzanne Stenzel, Theodora Fakles, Penny Fakles, and Janet George Taylor; I would like to express my appreciation for the patience and skill of Frederick A. Hetzel and Catherine Marshall at the University of Pittsburgh Press; and I would like to acknowledge my debt to three of my first teachers: Ralph Allen, Wandalie Henshaw, and Bert O. States. To Dr. States I owe special gratitude for I am constantly inspired by reading his work as these pages will show.

Rhythm in Drama

Introduction

Rhythm is an extremely difficult concept to pin down. Philosophers and aestheticians have wrestled with it and, in essence, acknowledged it the winner. Meanwhile artists and critics of the arts have been using the term somewhat unselfconsciously and even carelessly to describe the effect of a work or a part of a work. Indeed, *rhythm* is a term used frequently by theatre practitioners. Actors and directors work at the rhythm of a scene; they speak of the rhythms of Chekhov; critics of the drama describe certain scenes in terms of rhythmic impact. The term is often used quite accurately by those who have no wish to define it or to consider its aesthetic properties or to dwell upon its philosophical implications. However, it is often enough used inaccurately. The term is, to some users, synonymous with *tempo*. Richard Boleslavsky, who made rhythm the sixth of his first six lessons in acting, recognized that rhythm and tempo are often confused. He makes a charming distinction between the two concepts:

If Shakespeare had cast those two, he would have written:
> Rhythm—the Prince of Arts.
> Tempo—his bastard Brother.[1]

Anyone who has given special attention to rhythm finds, as Boleslavsky did, that rhythm is far more complex than tempo.

Tempo is simply a rate of speed. Rhythm is a whole pattern of organization.

Boleslavsky's discussion of rhythm, like the rest of his acting text, is deceptively whimsical and playful. Beneath the playfulness is evidence of the years of thought he gave to the subject of rhythm. His definition (which he intended for all the arts), he insists, is only a beginning. Rhythm is:

the orderly measurable changes of all the different elements comprised in a work of art—provided that all those changes progressively stimulate the attention of the spectator and lead invariably to the final aim of the artist.[2]

It is quite a good beginning because it provokes us to think about what rhythm is, but also to recognize what it is not. Boleslavsky, in focusing on change and progression, rejects the more common and less useful concern with musical meter. Meter is the basis of the definitions of two theatre artists— Constantin Stanislavsky and Alexander Dean—who talk about "units of equal length" and "beats and accents" but have difficulty relating the definiton to anything concrete in drama.[3]

Boleslavsky implies with his phrase "all the different elements" that the territory of rhythm is vast. And so it is. Other important concepts of this definition are that the changes in art are somehow orderly, not haphazard; that there is some progression in those changes which in turn leads the spectator along the right path; that at the end of the rhythmic progression is some final aim of the artist. All in all, Boleslavsky makes us wonder whether we are not closer to understanding the subject when we read Aristotle on action and Stanislavsky on objective since both writers are concerned with progressive change. It is at least easier to identify the orderly and measurable changes that Aristotle discusses and that Stanislavsky recommends to the actor than it is to assign a metrical count to a scene from dramatic literature.

Succeeding studies of rhythm are a good test of the basic soundness of Boleslavsky's definition. For instance, in 1953, the

French aesthetician Raymond Bayer published an essay, "The Essence of Rhythm," in which he discusses rather than defines rhythm. Bayer is more concerned with the visual than with the temporal arts. His discussion indicates that rhythm touches us emotionally, that it is basically an emotional force. The spectator has little personal identity in the presence of the art object: *"the aesthetic object must be envisaged as a strange composite of Self and Thing, a compound that appears initially and by its very nature inseparable."* The audience is captivated by art, or as Bayer describes it, perhaps even a bit mesmerized. And the force that captivates spectators and works emotional changes upon them is rhythm. Every aesthetic object is different and captivates differently, but in all of them "pulses of alternate storm and calm are based on a balanced dispersal of the stress, whatever graceful object we may be considering."[4]

Bayer's idea of alternate storm and calm is an important one, for it is not only an expression of change which reminds us of Boleslavsky's definition, but of a particular kind of change which can easily work an emotion on a spectator. The words *tension* and *release* might easily substitute for *storm* and *calm*— and several theorists have found alternating tension and release the substance of rhythm. Roger Sessions, who calls rhythm "the primary fact of music," explains:

The basic rhythmic fact is not the fact simply of alternation, but of a specific type of alternation with which we are familiar from the first movement of our existence as separate beings. We celebrate that event by drawing a breath, which is required of us if existence is to be realized. The drawing of the breath is an act of cumulation, of tension which is then released by the alternative act of exhalation.[5]

To Boleslavsky, Bayer, and Sessions, then, rhythm is to a great extent a product of orderly change. And rhythm has the power to work changes upon the audience. But how orderly are these changes? How "measurable," as Boleslavsky phrases it? Boleslavsky calls the changes in the color blue in Gainsborough's *Blue Boy* measurable because they were measured or created once, though they are nearly impossible to reproduce. Perhaps a better word for his *measurable* is *perceptible.* Bayer concentrates on the nonmeasurable aspect of art. It has "a numerical, though unconscious perfection. Numbers which we cannot know subtend the rhythms, and the rhythms are the bases of pleasure. *The plane of rhythmics, with its measure of feeling, is the locus of intersection of mathematicism and hedonism.*" Rhythm is *"the essence of art"* because *"what each and every aesthetic object imposes on us, in appropriate rhythms, is a unique and singular formula for the flow of our energy."*[6]

And does rhythm produce only emotional change in the spectator (as words like *storm* and *calm* would imply) or can rhythm in art produce other things as well—perceptions, ideas, questions? The answer seems to rest in how broad the definition of rhythm is. As its territory becomes more comprehensive, so do its powers. Kenneth Burke, who uses the word *rhythm* sparingly, but who deals often with the concept, shares with Bayer the idea that the spectator is in a kind of dream where the artist is the wizard or dream-maker. The artist is quite powerful. "He is the manipulator of blood, brains, heart, and bowels which, while we sleep, dictate the mould of our desires."[7] The recurring questions are first, How clear or perceptible do the changes in the art object have to be? and second, How awake or conscious of them does the audience have to be? Bayer's audience is mesmerized, Burke's is asleep, while the attention of Boleslavsky's spectator is being progressively stimulated by the changes in art. The only sensible answer is that we cannot know where stimulation ends, we cannot know how we know some things, we do not know how much we perceive subconsciously. We can only guess that the principles of what we *can* perceive or measure operate to some extent in what we do not or cannot consciously measure, that perception occurs both above and below the line of consciousness.

Suzanne Langer, like Roger Sessions, describes rhythm in terms of human physiology. She finds in heartbeat and breathing the alternating tensions and relaxations which are very basic examples of body rhythm. The important distinction between Langer's theory and others is that in her eyes rhythm consists not merely of tension and release but of *interdependent* tension and release. The alternating processes are dependent upon each other. "As we release the breath we have taken, we build up a bodily need of oxygen that is the motivation, and therefore the real beginning of the new breath," and "the diastole prepares the systole, and vice versa." Langer's major definition of rhythm is based upon this theory of preparation:

The essence of rhythm is the preparation of a new event by the ending of a previous one. A person who moves rhythmically need not repeat a single motion exactly. His movements, however, must be complete gestures, so that one can sense a beginning, intent, and consummation, and see in the last stage of one the condition and indeed the rise of another. Rhythm is the setting-up of new tensions by the resolution of former ones. They need not be of equal duration at all; but the situation that begets the new crisis must be inherent in the denouement of its forerunner.[8]

Langer looks to rhythm in both nature and in man-made things to help explain rhythm in art. The ticking of a watch or the fall, rise, and turning point of a pendulum she describes as rhythmic with equal measure; a bouncing ball rhythmic in unequal measure; and particularly impressive, the steady or regular breaking of waves. She explains an important concept with the example of breaking waves: "Each new comber rolling in is shaped by the undertow flowing back, and in its turn actually hurries the recession of the previous wave by suction. There is no dividing line between the two events. Yet a breaking wave is as definite an event as one could wish to find—a true dynamic *Gestalt*."[9]

All Langer's examples illustrate *balance* (or *opposition*, if we choose to inform the movement with conflict.) At any rate, tension balances relaxation, creation balances destruction. And interestingly, the balance is created by, or is a product of, proportionate expenditures of energy. The harder a ball is bounced the higher it goes in the air.

We learn early in life to expect balance in nature and in art. We wait for the answering gesture, the answering act, and the answering sound. We know that we, like most dramatic characters, want the opposite of what we possess at the moment. This is why it seems so natural that in Chekhov's *Three Sisters*, Olga, who is too busy, wants to relax while Irina, purposeless, cries for a project. We learn aphorisms to comfort ourselves: The bigger they are, the harder they fall. The grass always looks greener on the other side. When somebody cries somewhere, somebody will laugh somewhere else.

It is important to those studying drama to notice that tension and release are not only connected, but that they are connected in a paradoxical way. The dying wave, for example, is shaping the new wave, and the new wave is hurrying the death of the former wave. The investment of the pattern or cycle with meaning is part of Langer's system. Why else should she feel that a ticking watch is only rhythmic via our organizing interpretation? When I listen to my watch, I hear not an even or steady succession of beats, but a strong beat followed by three weaker beats. And that pattern repeated many times. I am probably not hearing accurately. Langer says we make units and accents where there are none. Is this the organizing interpretation that she speaks of? Or is it perhaps my insistence on *seeing* time go by as I *hear* the sameness of ticking? It is the point at which change carries with it meaning—ironic or paradoxical—that it becomes especially interesting to the actor, director, and critic. It perhaps even becomes especially rhythmic.

If it is difficult to separate meaning from rhythm in drama, it is because drama is filled with content and made of such specific materials. It is, as Kenneth Burke says, an information-giving art, much more confusing than music. With music it is easier to remember that form, and the psychology of form (another way of describing rhythm) rests in the audience. When a composer resolves or does not resolve a dissonance, he is making a choice which deals with audience psychology and audience desires.[10] He is setting up an expectation and either filling it or not. A playwright does the same thing with more content-oriented material. "Form is the creation of an appetite in the mind of the auditor, and the adequate satisfying of that appetite. This satisfaction—so complicated is the human mechanism —at times involves a temporary set of frustrations, but in the end these frustrations prove to be simply a more involved kind of satisfaction, and furthermore serve to make the satisfaction of fulfilment more intense."[11]

Definitions and discussions of rhythm, then, have several points in common. First, the audience is of primary importance: rhythm exists as it is perceived or felt by the audience. Second, the artist produces for the audience a set of expectations and (usually) fulfillments of those expectations. Third, rhythm involves some sort of alternation between opposites, generally producing a pattern of tensions and relaxations. Fourth, content is difficult to separate from rhythm: *what* produces storm and calm, tension and relaxation is important. Fifth, there is some order or pattern to the changes (perhaps not measurable). And sixth, there is an overall rhythm to a piece, an overall gesture or action that is imitated. Aristotle described the major rhythm as beginning, middle, and end. Langer's description of gesture is beginning, intent, and consummation. Boleslavsky insists that there is a progression and a final aim of the artist.

Much of the agreement about rhythm rests in two ideas: change and audience expectations. I cannot help but be reminded of H. W. Fowler's explanation of dramatic irony in *A Dictionary of Modern English Usage* because it is a way of dealing with audience expectations. Dramatic irony involves a remark made for two audiences, one of which will hear and not understand, the other of which will hear and understand, not only the remark, but also the first hearer's incomprehension. Every irony carries with it the expectation that it will be resolved. It does not hurt to remember that expectations are a form of tension and that resolutions offer at least a temporary release or relaxation. A good playwright, too, often makes the resolution the creator of a new tension. Dramatic irony is one of all the different elements which are part of a play's rhythm.

What part does irony, then, (not dramatic irony, though we might question the dramatic quality of all irony) play in a definition of rhythm? If irony involves the perception of opposites or the perception of the incongruous, the playwright and the audience operate as ironists much of the time. Rhythm might include the alternation of their roles from involvement to distance to involvement to distance.

Irony involves opposites, but so then does dialectic. Is there a place for the relation of dialectic to rhythm? Bert O. States devotes a good portion of his book, *Irony and Drama*, to the relation between irony and dialectic. Pure drama, "conceived as the strategy of developing conflicts by the rigorous inclusion of opposites," must include in some form dialectic and irony. States theorizes:

In sum, our formula—not, once again, for *all* plays but for drama as a mode of organization—would convert as follows: drama is the extension of oppositional development into the sphere of human action and passion; or as Burke might say, the dancing of the ironic-dialectical attitude. Whereas we think of irony as the agency of discovery of oppositions and contradiction in the "infinity of possibles" and dialectic as the ideological struggle waged by the possibles (dialectic equals irony explained), we would be most apt to use the word *drama*, or *dramatic*, when the struggle involves human action, or what Miss Langer would call Destiny (drama is irony acted out, or, if you wish, dialectic personified).[12]

If rhythm includes opposites, it must then include conflict and characterization or "dialectic personified."

Conflict, irony, and dialectic are only a few of the ways oppositions play themselves out in art. We should approach structure in a work of art in terms of "the *functioning* of a structure," says Kenneth Burke, and "the two main symbols for the charting of structural relationships would be the sign for 'equals'

and some such sign as the arrow ('from _____ to _____')."
Since literature is complex, and opposing principles are generally working together toward some end, *equals* is very close to
versus. Moreover, oppositions take two basic forms: polar otherness and synecdochic otherness. In polar otherness, things
which are opposite are united—heroism and villainy; in synecdochic otherness things which are different are united—the
house that represents the beloved is united with the beloved.[13]
Rhythm may indeed be as Bayer asserts, the place where mathematicism and hedonism meet. The usefulness of Burke's "formulas" is not the challenge to use them, but the challenge to remember that there are no simple formulas, that the elements in
a work of art are related and opposed in a variety of complex
ways. A key phrase that makes sense of his mathematics is "the
functioning of a structure." Indeed, that is perhaps the shortest
possible definition of rhythm. Burke is constantly aware that
each move or gesture an artist makes creates a desire for some
balancing gesture. The audience experiences some form of suspense, generally conceived of as the desire for some fact, but in
actuality much more far-reaching. It can be the desire for an
emotion or quality, a desire called forth by a preceding emotion
or quality. If a novelist makes the reader feel sultriness and oppression for several pages, that reader will want refreshment—
"a cold, fresh northwind" or some aspect of it.[14] That aspect
may be any analogue for a north wind.

Since order in the changes and progression in the changes
are part of a description of rhythm, the change (if the author
fulfills the reader's desire) from sultriness and oppression to a
cold, fresh, north wind is not yet rhythmically complete. It is *a*
change and not a pattern of changes. In a rhythmically complete work, the spectator perceives a pattern to the changes.
This observation can be applied to drama as easily as to the
novel. Indeed, one of the elements that narrative prose and
drama have in common is the implicit command to tell a story.
The story does not have to be full of external action. Beneath
the most uneventful or so-called static short stories, novels, and

plays (Chekhov, Beckett) are a series of patterned changes. And in both the story and the drama this presentation of a pattern of changes is different from the relation of one incident.

Edwin Peterson traditionally began his advanced writing seminar at the University of Pittsburgh with a reading of "The Litte Red Hen," in order to illustrate, he said, the difference between an incident and a story. If the little red hen had asked for help from her fellow barnyard creatures *once* and been refused *once* we would have had the relation of an incident, but not a story. A story includes the pattern (in this case, through repetition) of her conflict with the other animals. The basic elements of the story, as Peterson pointed out, were conflict, repetition, and change, elements which are present in some form in every work of literature. The important point here is that the incidents are not haphazard. There is a pattern to them.

The same is true of plays, of course. Even those plays which seem patternless. "All plays rely on patterning to some degree, since it is really through pattern that a work manages to repeat its idea; pattern, in other words, is pronounced rhythm."[15]

Rhythm is the force that describes the effect of a play on us. All the philosophers, aestheticians, and craftsmen who write about rhythm are describing this very process (and it is indeed a difficult one to describe), the process of *how* we are affected —moved to feel love, pity, anger, peace, resignation; *how* we are made to understand; *how* we are made to laugh and to cry.

Rhythm includes the functioning of structure, beats and accents, tension and release, inclusion of content, the preparation of new tensions, orderly measurable change, and mathematics. They make up this working definition of rhythm in drama:

The pattern or mathematics of a play in motion, functioning to produce in audiences a completed progression of physical, emotional, and intellectual responses by which they arrive at meaning. That pattern is recognizable through repetition and change of some element(s).

I believe that one of the most useful insights for critics and directors is that a great deal of the play—the groundwork for the mathematics—in each case is discernible from the first scene or the first few scenes at most. The playwright gives us the gameboard, the rules, and the pieces very early on. We might call that gameboard with its crucial accessories "the world of the play." Once the playwright has created that world, it is of necessity a limited world. The gameboard for Monopoly will allow you to win or lose real estate, but it will not allow you to get to the head of the class. The limited world of the play already carries with it certain expectations. Langer contends that once the rhythm is established, it dictates the rest of the play:

That rhythm is the "commanding form" of the play; it springs from the poet's original conception of the "fable," and dictates the major divisions of the work, the light or heavy style of its presentation, the intensity of the highest feeling and most violent act, the great or small number of characters, and the degrees of their development. The total action is a cumulative form; and because it is constructed by a rhythmic treatment of its elements, it appears to *grow* from its beginnings. That is the playwright's creation of "organic form."[16]

The playwright is the creator of this commanding form of the play. A good playwright sets the gears in motion and then plays as honest a game as possible with the audience. Pirandello gives us an excellent image of the playwright at work in his "Preface to *Six Characters in Search of an Author*." He says he could not honestly write the drama of the six characters who presented themselves to him and begged for life. Yet, bedeviled by these characters, he could not be rid of them. And so he wrote the drama of how he could *not* present them and their drama. Once he arrived at the conclusion that these characters were real, yet not real, acceptable, yet not acceptable—that they were, indeed, rejected stage characters—he discovered the world of the play: stage, actors, and characters. When he discovered the clash, interest, seduction, and resultant clash between art and life, he found the oppositions, and the rhythm, of the drama. In a sense the play needed only to be written after the important original conception. Pirandello explains that a self-conscious attempt to work out the play could never have succeeded as well as that one moment's inspiration which set the stage (the gameboard or the gears in motion, if you will). "The fact is that the play was really conceived in one of those spontaneous illuminations of the fantasy when by a miracle all the elements of the mind answer to each other's call and work in divine accord."[17]

The playwright, as creator or creative artist, gives us in words what will eventually appear before an audience. And a host of other artists will be instrumental in making the words on the page come alive for the audience. Among them are the scene designer, lighting designer, costume designer, director, and actors. All of them must be sensitive to rhythm (the playwright's rhythm) and must use rhythm in their respective arts.

Of course each can alter the playwright's rhythm by superimposing changes that the playwright did not intend. But it is in trying to sense the playwright's patterning that a production team recognizes the wholeness that Langer describes as organic form. By concentrating on what the playwright has written, we become more aware, I think, of what Langer means when she defines drama as poetry. "Once we recognize that drama is neither dance nor literature, nor a democracy of various arts functioning together, but is poetry in the mode of action, the relations of all its elements to each other and to the whole work become clear."[18]

And so all discussions of rhythm in this book will be focused on dramatic action or *changes* based upon the interaction of characters. I will be concerned, too, with how a playwright writes visual as well as aural rhythm. I will be looking for poetry in the mode of action.

Many of the passages I will discuss are very well known. The reason for this is obvious. If we can apprehend the principles of rhythm that operate in what we are familiar with, we can more easily transfer those principles to other works. Again, the rhythm of an isolated line is not the business of this book. The *exchanges* which are analyzed generally manifest a major principle of organization in the whole work from which they are taken.

Several works will be dealt with in translation, notably plays by Ibsen and Chekhov. My concern in each case is not the nuance of language, but the pattern of exchanges which most actors, directors, and critics (for whom this book is intended) will deal with only in English. Examples from Chekhov are taken from the translation by Constance Garnett for which I have a personal preference, precisely because I like its sense of rhythm. (It may be argued forever that no translator can accurately catch something so elusive and subtle as rhythm in changing the words and structures from one language to another. The translator is always part adaptor. For me, the language of the Garnett translation complements the structure of the plays. And I have been assured by more than one fluent reader of Russian that Garnett is—word for word—especially faithful to the original.) It borders on the unwise to discuss the "rhythm of dramatic action" and to bypass Chekhov who practically popularized the notion.

Much of the time, a discussion of rhythm will sound like (and be related to) a discussion of dramatic action, plotting, conflict, or irony. Such relationships are necessary because rhythm plays itself out through all these elements. Why then, if rhythm bears such a close relationship to everything else, deal with it at all? I think it is worth talking about because it is related to all other elements of drama, but not synonymous with any of them; it is most closely related to pattern or form, for it is pattern in motion, or form as it functions; and when human beings cease to be interested in how and why they are moved to think, feel, and react to life, and critics cease to be interested in how and why an artist moves them in a particular way, the world will have stopped moving.

It is fascinating to catch some glimpse of how a clock works, an experience almost every child has, and with that knowledge comes some appreciation of the making of a clock. A play is in its way a much more precise instrument than a clock. Each play exists to inspire great numbers of people to disassemble it, not just to study it, but to re-create it in production. The better we understand the workings of rhythm, the movement of a play, the better that re-creation can be.

The Open Scene:
Meanings Through Rhythm

Sometimes the best way of understanding a phenomenon is by examining it in its most pared-down form. The infinite varieties and complexities of rhythm in drama may be better appreciated by inspecting rhythmic dialogue first in its more obvious forms. Many of the following observations may seem blatantly clear, but they are necessary foundations for the investigation of more complex or subtle rhythmic manifestations.

The following dialogue, known as an open scene, is one of a number of similar scripts given as an assignment to beginning students of acting and directing. They are asked to make sense of it by performing it in four different ways, each of which is a complete and perfectly understandable playlet. The scene is so open that playlets have been performed about everything from abstract emotional losses to bank robbery. Students of directing are asked to invent scenes in the style of Ibsen, in the style of Chekhov, or of Tennessee Williams or Beckett. Here is the dialogue:

1. Oh
2. Yes
1. Why are you doing this
2. It's the best thing
1. You can't mean it
2. No, I'm serious
1. Please

2. What
1. What does this mean
2. Nothing
1. Listen
2. No
1. So different
2. Not really
1. Oh
2. You're quite good
1. Forget it
2. What
1. Go
2. I will[1]

Obviously, under normal circumstances, a great deal of "visual drama" has to be added to this dialogue. Setting, costuming, properties, and lighting can help to give the scene meaning. For instance, in one serious scene in the "Ibsen style," a quite emotionally contained husband and wife discussed the necessity of ridding their house of the last reminders of their son who died as an infant. The full meaning of the scene was directly dependent upon visual elements: the composure of the wife was evidently a composure covering a high degree of emotionality by the *way* she read a book; the ambivalence underlying the decision to get rid of the reminders was evident from the careful handling of the box that held the items and the even more careful handling of the items within the box. The weakening of resolve on the part of the wife, the continued insistence on the part of the husband were evident through the blocking of the scene. Visual elements have to be of importance in an open scene. In another scene, a "Tennessee Williams style" playlet, the bottles, glasses, cleaning rag, and clock of a barroom, as well as the suitcase and wedding band of the man who was leaving his wife, were of vast significance in telling the story of a sentimental exchange between two strangers late one night.

Do the words of this open scene, then, mean anything at all? They certainly at first glance seem to mean nothing. Indeed, these twenty almost style-less lines leave much to be desired as dramatic dialogue. Although this open scene must be made to have specific meanings (and it has had hundreds in classroom assignments), it already as a skeleton has *some* meaning. It is an excellent exercise in rhythm with minimal content.

First of all it gives us a simple pulse by a somewhat regular alternation of speaker. The lengths of the speeches are not quite equal, which makes the pulse vary a bit and adds interest. Conflict is apparent in that the responses of Character 2 run counter to those of Character 1. And if the lines are given their most conventional interpretations, each character begins to take on some consistency of response. The lines of Character 1 are more aggressive: "Why are you doing this—You can't mean it—Please—What does this mean—Listen—So different." This character speaks in questions and pleas indicating a more open attitude. Character 2, on the other hand, seems more resistive and defensive: "It's the best thing—No, I'm serious—What—Nothing—No—Not really." Most of these responses are statements and negatives.

The potential conflict might be phrased thus: Character 1 wants something from Character 2, either information, or something more concrete. Perhaps Character 1 even wants to make an impression on Character 2. Character 2 is resisting Character 1 on some issue. Since something must happen on stage, a change must take place (or it must *not* take place, giving us to understand that though other things change, the major change we were expecting cannot happen). At any rate the action must pass through some sort of crisis in which there is a change of pattern, even if momentary. The crisis, as testing point, points the action by showing us the moment in which the situation will change, if it is ever going to change. In productions of this open scene, this point seems to fall fairly consistently at "So different —Not really—Oh." A crisis at this point is natural because the three lines mark a change in pattern, or at least a possible change. We sense that this is a changing point because what happens afterward is different. If we stick to conventional readings and meanings (ruling out sarcasm and irony for the moment), it is evident that Character 2 is changed with "You're quite good." For one thing, no matter what the tone, the word "you" indicates that Character 2 recognizes Character 1 in a more direct fashion than previously.

In addition to providing a pulse and a potential conflict, the dialogue also provides several possibilities for clustering or grouping the lines. And the clustering of lines will point eventually to meanings, because the patterning or grouping of thoughts and actions (the overall ordering of the pulse) is rhythm. There are several points at which change might take place. The rhythm of the whole varies in relation to internal change patterns. Here are two of the dominant possibilities:

Oh	Oh
Yes	Yes
	Why are you doing this
Why are you doing this	It's the best thing
It's the best thing	You can't mean it
You can't mean it	No, I'm serious
No, I'm serious	
	Please
Please	What
What	What does this mean
	Nothing
What does this mean	Listen
Nothing	No
Listen	
No	So different
	Not really
So different	Oh
Not really	You're quite good
	Forget it
Oh	What
	Go
You're quite good	I will
Forget it	
What	
Go	
I will	

In the first variation, the maximum amount of breakup is used (2-4-2-4-2-1-2-1-2 pattern). Breakup tends to give the scene emotional, not to mention psychological, qualities. The first pattern capitalizes on most possible changes while retaining a sense of order. Order is possible because the changes are related. The tentative quality of "Oh—Yes" is matched by a similarly tentative quality in "Please—What." These weaker expressions are contrasted with the more definite qualities of lines like "You can't mean it—No, I'm serious," lines which imply a more open confrontation. The second variation is much like the first, except that while the first gives the impression of repeated avoidance-confrontation-avoidance-confrontation, the second streamlines (makes classical) the confrontation by dividing it into three equal parts, each of which encompasses similar smaller changes.

A third variation, more streamlined than the second, is ironically a less "finished" and more "irregular" rhythm. It involves simply splitting the scene in two:

Oh
Yes
Why are you doing this
It's the best thing
You can't mean it
No, I'm serious
Please
What
What does this mean
Nothing

Listen
No
So different
No really
Oh
You're quite good
Forget it
What

Go
I will

Because each section includes a wider variety of responses, the whole scene takes on a somewhat offbeat, tired-out flavor, perhaps not unlike the two-act circular dramas of Beckett. Whereas a three-part change feels the most conventional and comfortable (perhaps we have learned it from three-part fairy tales) a two-part change feels at once too neat and too incomplete. An artist like Beckett can make use of that double impression.

The indicators of rhythm in the open scene are, as Boleslavsky says, its orderly and measurable changes. When many changes are pointed up, we tend to be aware of the relationships between the changes, as in the first variation. Emotion seems to guide the changes. With fewer changes and more streamlining, in the second pattern, we are made much more aware of progression. The playlet seems to take on cause-effect patterning. The three-part pattern may be precisely what Aristotle was describing as beginning, middle, and end, for he implies, at least, a playing out of a causally arranged pattern. The changes that guide the progression seem to proceed from variations in strategy. Much more difficult to describe is the effect of the third variation. The change seems arbitrary, a pattern imposed on the action, since nothing is resolved at first, and then *something* seems to be resolved rather quickly. A change of tone might be the motivating factor that makes each half cohere, for example, a serious to comic or comic to serious tone change on the part of the participants.

The indicators of rhythm, then, seem to be changes, but the stability of a rhythmic pattern depends upon consistency. The stabilizers of rhythm appear to be consistency of character attitude (e.g., Character 2's negative responses), consistency of goal though strategy varies (e.g., Character 1 might try several tacks to get cooperation from Character 2), and consistency of change itself (e.g., it occurs regularly and for the same reasons).

In any rhythmic pattern something(s) must remain stable while other things must change. So far we have discussed only three patterns on a set script and only three of the commonest methods of measuring change in dialogue. Kenneth Burke, in his "Lexicon Rhetoricae," describes rhythmic variations in a prose sentence as a product of "differentiations [which] are based on logical groupings." What he says of the sentence is applicable to a whole passage or indeed to a whole work. He attests to the fact that there is a mathematicism about rhythm as well as a sense of artistic individuality: "The logical groupings upon which the rhythmic differentiations are based will differ with the individual, not only as to the ways in which he conceives a sentence's relationships, but also as to their number—and much of the 'individuality' in a particular prose style could be traced to the number and nature of the author's logical groupings."[2]

The rhythmic variations on the open scene which have been discussed so far have depended upon fairly serious and conventional readings of the lines. However, since the lines of the scene are capable of many interpretations, let us look briefly at two further variations. If, for instance, the lines of Character 1 are read as fearful and defensive questions (instead of goal-oriented aggressive questions) and those of Character 2 are read as threatening lines (aggressive rather than resistive responses), not only does the rhythm change, but so does the style—to melodrama or comedy, depending upon how seriously we take the threats of Character 2 and the fear of Character 1. As a melodrama (suppose 2 is going to kill 1), the changes will be more gradual and in some senses more subtle to maintain the tension. One cannot afford to release mounted tension with broad changes in either tragedy or melodrama, for laughter is the usual result. As a comedy (suppose 2 is trying to seduce 1), the changes will be bigger and will be emphasized. Release is the mechanism of comedy. Interestingly enough though, no matter what tone is imposed upon the open scene, the places in the script for *possible* change remain the same. And so does the consistency of responses from character. Rhythm is so delicate a thing that any one change, either in tempo or the pointing of changes or the size of changes, causes a new relationship of the parts to each other and is capable, therefore, of altering style, tone, and meaning.

Style itself and the pattern of speaker alternation are two important factors in indicating a rhythm of dialogue. Both have been passed over rather quickly in the discussion of the open scene. The pattern of speaker alternation in the open scene is not a particularly interesting one although it does provide a pulse, regular though it is, for the action. And although it is easy to call the open scene style-less, it cannot be wholly so for we might describe it as terse, or lacking in images, or even spare. Another great maker of rhythm, as well as a signpost to rhythm, is sound or word repetition. For example, in Petruchio's "Kate" speech and Othello's "Farewell" speech, word repetition is so obvious that an audience is consciously aware of it. The repeated words are so arranged that they point to the major changes of the speech. The minute specifics of exactly how this is done might consitute a few chapters in a book on prosody. But we can at least be aware of the power of repeated sounds, words, and phrases to beat a pulse and move us at the same time. An examination of several examples of sound repetition and a few observations on what we are likely to think and feel as a result of them is the subject of the next section. The open scene, however, does not capitalize on repeated words. Although some words are repeated eventually, like "oh" and "no," they do not call attention to themselves as repetitions. At best, the rhymed effect of oh–no–no–so–oh–go provides a rhythmic progression, with, interestingly, Character 1 starting and finishing the progression with rhymes of Character 2's repetition of "No." There is also an association of sounds in Character 2's negatives: no–nothing–no–not. These are really hidden effects; they are not immediately obvious as are the "Kate" of Petruchio or the "Farewell" of Othello.

The devices for better understanding the rhythmic possibilities of the open scene are the very same devices we use to substantiate an emotion or an impression in life. If we have just met someone who we think has a wonderful sense of humor, we often go on to describe *how* (Boleslavsky's magic word for rhythm) we got the impression. We might say, for instance, that every time A or B spoke, our wit "turned everything they said around." We are describing verbal strategy and to some extent speaker alternation. We might say, "he turned a dull evening into a gradually more and more pleasant one." We would be describing progression and the timing of change. Kenneth Burke, in his discussion of significant form, utilizes an example from life to explain how form or repetition of some principle accents or emphasizes a particular meaning. Form does exist in life, and all our basic training for understanding it comes from observing ourselves and our fellows in varying contexts. Here Burke is talking about a repetition and progression from life—a conversation between a boy and girl—which produced a comic effect:

Pointing to a field beyond the road, the boy asked: "Whose field is that?" The girl answered: "That is Mr. Murdock's field"—and went on to tell where Mr. Murdock lived, how many children he had, when she had last seen these children, which of them she preferred, but the boy interrupted: "What does he do with the field?" He usually plants the field in rye, she explained; why, only the other day he drove up with a wagon carrying a plough, one of his sons was with him, they left the wagon at the gate, the two of them unloaded the plough, they hitched the—but the boy interrupted severely: "Does the field go all the way over to the brook?" The conversation continued in this vein, always at cross-purposes, and growing increasingly humorous to eavesdroppers as its formal principle was inexorably continued.[3]

Burke goes on to illustrate varying uses of the cross-purposes principle for serious, sentimental, and ironic effects. Although he does not title this part of his study "Rhythm," here as everywhere he is describing rhythmic effects, for his eye is constantly on pattern in motion.

Life does not generally order itself as neatly as art orders its vision of life, but the principles of understanding life, when we are not too involved in it to observe, are the same principles that we use in understanding art. Matters of taste, personal philosophy, and varying interpretations aside, when we are in a noticing mood, there are certain principles of conversation which strike us, as the cross-purposes of the boy and girl struck Burke. He might have analyzed it thus: the boy asked brief questions in which progression was the keynote; the girl gave long answers in which digression was the keynote.

Suppose we overhear in a restaurant a rather personal conversation. A man is telling his date all her faults. He is aggressively listing the problems with "her personality." He tells her she is lazy, she never makes a decision on her own, she always believes other people are right, she is not discriminating about people, she likes everyone too much. The woman (at intervals) weakly agrees with him. We might later describe the conversation by naming one or all of the elements which repeat: (1) speaker alternation patterns—the man consistently talked more, for longer periods than the woman did; (2) positive and negative charges—he was talking energetically *for* change *to* her and *about* her, while she remained in a secondary or receiver position; (3) verbal strategy—the man used blunt generalizations, the woman continued to agree with him, her agreement only seemed to spur him on to more blunt generalizations; (4) repetition of words—the man with some regularity patterned phrases by repeating "always, always, always, never never, never"; (5) style or overall patterning—neither party seemed to care about overhearers, but delivered their dialogue in a vulgarly exhibitionistic manner.

The point I am trying to make is that we notice the repetitions of words, strategies, attitudes, lengths of speeches, and so on. We also notice any changes in the patterns and we also look for or expect progressions. If the woman's answers become more strained, we predict trouble for the couple. If the man's tirades gradually diminish in length, all other things remaining equal, we might assume he is wearing out his repertoire. If the woman gets progressively more cheerful while the man hysterically repeats her faults, we might assume that she has her own methods of retaliating, and they will, as usual, end in a draw to repeat their scene in another restaurant next week. At any rate, it is the patterns of repetition, change, and progression that tell the story. Though many unwilling audience members in a restaurant might come up with different reactions to the scene— "touchingly communicative," "embarrassing," "comic"—the playwright's job is to lure willing overhearers to a particular conclusion by carefully patterning and emphasizing particular changes. The restaurant scene is too unstructured to unite a mass of listeners in a common point of view and move them toward a common perception. To the best of playwrights this is a difficult task, one which is impossible to achieve fully.

The following chapters examine in more detail the kinds of rhythm listed above. The rhythm of good dramatic dialogue is complex because it is made up of many minor, complementary rhythms. Northrop Frye discusses four rhythmic patterns in the line "Aye, but to die and go we know not where."[4] A first inspection of a passage of dramatic dialogue for "its rhythm" can be staggering. One gets the impression that rhythm can be felt, but not isolated or discussed. And indeed, many a writer has insisted upon the difficulty of dealing with the concept. Rather than take a passage and look for "its rhythm," I have chosen to deal with several known manifestations of rhythm and to cite various passages in which each kind is exemplified. My aim is to illustrate as well as possible the relationship of the specific pattern to other rhythmic patterns in the play. Categories may sometimes seem arbitrary, and indeed they overlap at times. For example, repetition of verbal strategy is an element of style. But the categories—repetition of verbal strategy and repetition of stylistic devices—deal with separate focuses. Therefore they represent different ways of perceiving rhythm. The former refers to some motivated behavior on the part of a character or characters—a way of proceeding to get what they want. The latter refers to our awareness of the author's voice (his word choice, volume, inflection patterns)—how *he* goes about saying what he has to say and getting the response he wants. Naturally he does it through his characters, but his voice underlies all of theirs.

There may be more classifications for the ways we perceive rhythm in dialogue. But it seems to me that any other category is very much related to one that I have chosen to discuss. Whole books might be devoted to the differences between verse and prose dialogue. And there are of course the obvious differences: verse allows for metrical order, lends a sense of formality, generally lends more dignity or grandeur to the words, is not as "realistic," and so forth. However, there are rhythmic patterns which because they are *dramatic rhythms* apply to both verse and prose dialogue; these are the patterns with which I will be primarily concerned, for they point to the dramatic action of a play through interaction of characters.

Repetition of Sounds, Words, and Phrases

How do we know when a playwright is repeating words for rhythmic effect? A single word or phrase which recurs only twice is not likely to be noticed by us. In other words, it is not used as a device for beating out a rhythm. Indeed, repetition of a word or phrase is probably the most common device in playwriting because it makes clear a movement from one character's response to another's. Generally, a linear progression results from chaining words. For instance, in act 1 of Ibsen's *The Wild Duck*, Gregers Werle moves the confrontation with Old Werle by repeating his father's words. By doing so, Gregers not only points up the important words, but also makes clear his own dissection of any words which give his father protection:

WERLE. . . . . You may take my word for it, Gregers, I have done all I could without positively laying myself open to all sorts of suspicion and gossip—

GREGERS. Suspicion—? Oh, I see.

WERLE. I have given Ekdal copying to do for the office, and I pay him far, far more for it than his work is worth—

GREGERS (*without looking at him*). H'm; that I don't doubt.

WERLE. You laugh? Do you think I am not telling you the truth? Well, I certainly can't refer you to my books, for I never enter payments of that sort.

GREGERS (*smiles coldly*). No, there are certain payments it is best to keep no account of.

WERLE (*taken aback*). What do you mean by that?
GREGERS (*mustering up courage*). Have you entered what it cost you to
  have Hialmar Ekdal taught photography?
WERLE. I? How "entered" it?   (P. 84)[1]

The chaining of words keeps the scene moving, certainly. An
interesting additional point is Gregers' splitting of the simple
phrase "enter payments" into a veiled accusation about payments, followed by an ironic question using "entered." The
word-chaining process appears with only minor variations in
different translations, for instance, "expenses" for "payments."[2] The passage serves as a good illustration of a logical
progression by a playwright who was a master of the technique.

But suppose a playwright repeats a word or phrase three
times, four times, or even more in a tightly recurring pattern.
What is the effect? Pinter opens his one-act play *A Slight Ache*
with a repetition so obvious that it immediately catches our attention and makes us suspect that the world of the play we have
just entered is too patterned to be realistic (italics added):

FLORA. Have you noticed the *honeysuckle* this morning?
EDWARD. The what?
FLORA. The *honeysuckle*.
EDWARD. *Honeysuckle*? Where?
FLORA. By the back gate, Edward.
EDWARD. Is that *honeysuckle*? I thought it was . . . *convolvulus*, or some-
  thing.
FLORA. But *you know* it's *honeysuckle*.
EDWARD. I tell you I thought it was *convolvulus*.
    (*Pause.*)[3]

There is consistency in the words repeated in that both are
flowers. There is consistency in Flora's telling Edward about
the flowers, and consistency as well in Edward's questioning indifference. There is change, however, when Edward introduces
a new accent, *convolvulus*—a second odd-sounding word, syllables longer than all others with the exception of its cousin,
honeysuckle. When Edward makes his introduction, he does so

hesitantly, and his hesitation leads to a somewhat tense confrontation (honeysuckle against convolvulus), followed by a pause. This first progression, which ends in tension and a pause, is mirrored by the second progression. The second unit or dramatic "build" picks up the repetitions of the first and elaborates on them, this time taking on more comic overtones as Edward, slapped once, comes back for more:

FLORA. It's in wonderful *flower*.

EDWARD. I must look.

FLORA. The whole garden's in *flower* this morning. The clematis. The *convolvulus*. Everything. I was out at seven. I stood by the pool.

EDWARD. Did you say—that the *convolvulus* was in *flower*?

FLORA. Yes.

EDWARD. But good God, you just denied there was any.

FLORA. I was talking about the *honeysuckle*.

EDWARD. About the what?

FLORA *(calmly)*. Edward—*you know* that shrub outside the toolshed.

EDWARD. Yes, yes.

FLORA. That's *convolvulus*.

EDWARD. That?

FLORA. Yes.

EDWARD. Oh.

    (Pause.)

  I thought it was *japonica*.

FLORA. Oh, good Lord no.

EDWARD. Pass the teapot, please.

    (Pause. She pours tea for him.)

  I don't see why I should be expected to distinguish between these plants. It's not my job.

FLORA. *You know* perfectly well what grows in your garden.

EDWARD. Quite the contrary. It is clear that I don't.

    (Pause.)   (Pp. 9–10)

Utilizing words that relate to those in the first progression, Pinter beats his rhythm out again, this time, however, building to a pause before Edward's "I thought it was japonica." Edward's admission of his lack of knowledge is comic, because it is a beat late—timed after a pause—and because it is a crisp repetition of "I thought it was convolvulus or something." The line is a perfect example of what is generally called understatement, a device often used with Edward's sort of crispness in the British comedy of manners. And although the first build led to a somewhat threatening exchange about knowledge and left us with an uneasy chuckle, we might almost at this point believe we are in the world of Noel Coward. But we are not allowed to remain there for long. The build almost seems to force itself on. In answer to Edward's "Pass the teapot, please," Flora pours for him. Suddenly Pinter puts us back in time by repeating the threatening comments about what Edward does or does not know. It is not a word for word repetition but the exchange is clearly the same. Pinter, by forcing the repetition, has made it quite evident that the world of Edward and Flora is in some way strangely precarious. In case any doubt is left, Pinter gives us another repetition from the past and yet another reference following it to the fact that nature spells only peril to Edward:

FLORA *(rising)*. I was up at seven. I stood by the pool. The peace. And everything in flower. The sun was up. You should work in the garden this morning. We could put up the canopy.
EDWARD. The canopy? What for?
FLORA. To shade you from the sun.
EDWARD. Is there a breeze?
FLORA. A light one.
EDWARD. It's very treacherous weather, *you know*.
    (Pause.) (P. 10)

The tone has changed several times, but the odds are on the threatening atmosphere. William L. Sharp in *Language in Drama* describes Pinter's people as ones "continually changing direction." Within so small a unit as a line, they move "from attack to defense, from affection to dislike, from invitation to rejection," although the reason for that change cannot be found "within that line or within the action that precedes the line. . . . The only reason we assume a change has taken place is that the tone of a conversation has changed. We can at best guess at the reason for its change."[4] We may only be able to guess at reasons, but the changes are taking direction. The meanings are in the progressions, sensible or not. There are other consistencies in the progressions in addition to their habit of ending on a vaguely threatening note. After each pause, for instance, the characters do a kind of backtracking to a previous statement or reference. In other words, they do not go forward, but instead paraphrase an old sore point. A second characteristic of the progression is that the number of pauses is increasing, or pauses are becoming more frequent. As each section of dialogue becomes somewhat shorter than we might expect, the conflict seems almost worn-out, giving us the sense of old gripes unresolved. Pinter's pauses are, in the most formal sense, preparing us for the subsequent action of the play. They are rhythmic in themselves and might be translated in terms of their frequency (by the length of the scenes between) as beat-beat-pause, beat-beat-beat-beat-pause, beat-pause, beat-pause, beat-beat-pause. In addition to their regulating rhythm, they are pointing to a larger pattern which describes the whole play.

Pinter describes his use of pauses or silences as they are related to sounds: "There are two silences. One when no word is spoken. The other when perhaps a torrent of language is being employed. This speech is speaking of a language locked beneath it. That is its continual reference. The speech we hear is an indication of that we don't hear. It is a necessary avoidance, a violent, sly, anguished or mocking smoke-screen which keeps the other in its place. When true silence falls, we are still left with echo but are near nakedness. One way of looking at speech is to say it is a constant strategem to cover nakedness."[5] *A Slight Ache* is good evidence that Pinter is explaining very accurately his own particular use of pauses. The silences with which he fills the first part of his play are repeated in two analogous ways as the play continues. No word is uttered by the strange, forbidding figure of the Matchseller, a character who embodies silence. And the torrents of words spoken by both Edward and Flora to the Matchseller—privately, out of hearing of each other—are very much the speeches of silence which Pinter describes. If the silences seem to be increasing early in the play, they increase to such a point that the final two-thirds of the stage time might be described as primarily silence, punctuated by short bursts of conflict between Edward and Flora.

If the pause is a rhythmic element, what function does the language of repeated words serve? Each set of repetitions is used to point up conflict before each pause. Pinter has made introduction of a new subject equal conflict. Edward changes the subject to convolvulus: tension. Edward changes the subject from convolvulus to japonica: tension. Edward changes the subject from the sun to the breeze: tension. The repetitions, themselves, give us the sense that Edward and Flora are going back to square one. Square one is not terribly comfortable, since the briefness of the sentences and phrases makes each line itself seem to be clothed in silence. A period, or any halting punctuation for that matter, indicates a pause, if minimal. And Pinter has punctuated his dialogue liberally. For instance in Flora's substantially repeated "up at seven" speech, a speech which mirrors a previous one, an added sense of repetition is achieved by the briefness of the lines: "I was up at seven. I stood by the pool. The peace. And everything in flower. The sun was up." The speeches become a little longer when she makes more direct contact with Edward: "You should work in the garden this morning. We could put up the canopy." This speech, like the others, calls attention to itself—not so much because of what it means but because of how it is phrased. Questions are provoked because of *how* things are phrased. The fact that there are no clear answers is part of Pinter's meaning. There are no explanations for why Flora insists that Edward knows what his garden possesses. We may surmise that it is because he refuses to know. There is no explanation for Edward's conviction that the weather is treacherous. Possibly because Flora wants him to be out in the garden. If Pinter had explanations in mind, he might have written that Edward caught cold easily or that the wind lowered the temperature by ten degrees, but Pinter is not in an answer-giving frame of mind.

He is, however, in a symbol-giving frame of mind. And the word repetitions point to the symbols. A constant is Flora's nature-loving (flora-loving) talk. (She speaks of nothing else.) She seems to be trying to lure Edward into her world—either by seducing him or threatening him. She either says "Everything is wonderful here" or "*You know* you're resisting me." Constant, too, is Edward's avoidance of Flora's world through (pretended?) lack of knowledge and lack of interest. This from a man who is, we eventually learn, a scholar and who is capable of passionate interest in a number of subjects—so long as he can examine them from a distance. The eventual playing out of the symbolic conflict and its resultant ironies is not the subject of the moment, however. The fact that the rhythmic repetitions lead us to the symbols as well as to the conflict is important. Rhythm, or pattern in motion, is a clue to meaning.

When rhythmic dialogue is unmistakably evident through word repetitions, when rhythm imposes itself upon the conscious mind of the spectator, particularly at the start of the play, it obviously affects his subsequent perceptions. In the case of *A Slight Ache,* form is imposed on Pinter's nightmarish world by the rhythmic dialogue. The dialogue prepares us for the nightmare and distances us from it at the same time, allowing comedy, admittedly dark. Bergson says that when we are distanced observers of the *"mechanical encrusted on the living,"*[6] we are in a position to laugh. Since Pinter's rhythm is beat out so insistently through sound repetition, we are to some extent mesmerized by it, mesmerized to accept a world which is at the same time vaguely threatening and nightmarishly patterned. The hypnotic or mesmerizing effect of heavily repetitive dialogue is an interesting phenomenon. We are apt to be lulled by obvious repetition, lulled into accepting and believing the unacceptable and the unbelievable. Northrop Frye, in describing the sound recurrences of poetry, suggests a possible effect of recurrence in dramas like Pinter's. The root of the effect, he says, is "*charm*: . . . the hypnotic incantation that, through its pulsing dance rhythm, appeals to involuntary physical response, and is hence not far from the sense of magic, or physically compelling power. The etymological descent of charm from *carmen*, song, may be noted. Actual charms have a quality that is imitated in popular literature by work songs of various kinds, especially lullabies, where the drowsy sleep-inducing repetition shows the underlying oracular or dream pattern very clearly."[7] Of course, rhythmic repetition can provide more than one effect, as Frye notes, but one of its prevalent effects is a mesmerizing one. Advertisers have learned this lesson well, to our disadvantage. Pinter has learned the method very well himself, and before he shocks us, he lures us into a patterned world in which the shocks can be experienced through a sedative of words. Besides, when words are so often repeated, they (ironically) become less important and less effective in terms of specific meanings, and more important in terms of their place in a pattern.

Edward Albee's *A Delicate Balance*, appropriately titled, is a play less symmetrical than *A Slight Ache*. The opening dialogue here, too, is so rhythmically patterned that it calls attention to itself. Because it intrudes upon our consciousness *as* rhythm, it prepares us for a world somewhat surreal, a world pared down to a single emotion (fear) and a single strategy (escape). We know we have entered such a world because of Agnes's long opening speech which is almost a monologue. It is extremely and obviously patterned.

The first thing that comes to our attention, here, as in *A Slight Ache*, is the repetition of single words and phrases. It is an interesting exercise in mood and tone to extract the repeated words and read them as if they comprised a very offbeat and abstract poem, which is not really far from the case: astonishing-belief-surprise-belief-surprising-belief-adrift-adrift-drifting-go mad-anisette-go adrift-astonishing-speculation-go mad-anisette-cognac-speculation-speculate-go quite mad-ribbons-cognac-adrift-cognac-mad-ribbons-ribbon-astonishes-fear-fear-speculation-astonishing.

Albee tells us in stage directions that Agnes is wistful, and her recurring words certainly support such a mood. It seems, however, that when a playwright forces us to notice a pattern, he is doing so for a reason, that there is, in other words, more pattern than the obvious. By producing an odd pattern in motion or an odd rhythm Albee has forced us to notice, consciously or not, that it takes Agnes nearly three full pages of printed dialogue to finish a thought. Between her first and last "What I find most astonishing" is a digression of considerable length. When she finally finishes the thought she began with her first line, she finishes the first build or unit of the play and provides a major accent: Claire. Minor accents, as well as minor patterns, exist in this scene to support the major pattern. But first an examination of the scene itself:

> (In the library-livingroom. AGNES in a chair, TOBIAS at a shelf, looking into cordial bottles.)
>
> AGNES (speaks usually softly, with a tiny hint of a smile on her face: not sardonic, not sad . . . wistful, maybe). What I find most astonishing— aside from that belief of mine, which never ceases to surprise me by the very fact of its surprising lack of unpleasantness, the belief that I might very easily—as they say—lose my mind one day, not that I suspect I am about to, or am even . . . nearby . . .
>
> TOBIAS (he speaks somewhat the same way). There is no saner woman on earth, Agnes (putters at the bottles).
>
> AGNES. . . . for I'm not that sort; merely that it is not beyond . . . happening; some gentle loosening of the moorings sending the balloon adrift —and I think that is the only outweighing thing: adrift; the . . . becoming a stranger in . . . the world, quite . . . uninvolved, for I never see it as violent, only a drifting—what are you looking for, Tobias?
>
> TOBIAS. We will all go mad before you. The anisette.
>
> AGNES (a small happy laugh). Thank you, darling. But I could never do it —go adrift—for what would become of you? Still, what I find most astonishing, aside, as I said, from that speculation—and I wonder, too, sometimes, if I am the only one of you to admit to it: not that I may go mad, but that each of you wonders if each of you might not—why on earth do you want anisette?
>
> TOBIAS (considers). I thought it might be nice.
>
> AGNES (wrinkles her nose). Sticky. I will do cognac. It is supposed to be healthy—the speculation, or the assumption, I suppose, that if it oc-

curs to you that you might be, then you are not; but I've never been much comforted by it; it follows, to my mind, that since I speculate I might, some day, or early evening I think more likely—some autumn dusk—go quite mad, then I very well might. *(bright laugh)* Some autumn dusk: Tobias at his desk, looks up from all those awful bills, and sees his Agnes, mad as a hatter, chewing ribbons on her dress. . . .

TOBIAS *(pouring)*. Cognac?

AGNES. Yes; Agnes Sit-by-the-fire, her mouth full of ribbons, her mind aloft, adrift; nothing to do with the poor old thing but put her in a bin somewhere, sell the house, move to Tucson, say, and pine in the good sun, and live to be a hundred and four. *(He gives her her cognac.)* Thank you, darling.

TOBIAS *(kisses her forehead)*. Cognac is sticky, too.

AGNES. Yes, but it's nicer. Sit by me, hm?

TOBIAS *(does so; raises his glass)*. To my mad lady, ribbons dangling.

AGNES *(smiles)*. And, of course, I haven't worn the ribbon dress since Julia's remarriage. Are you comfortable?

TOBIAS. For a little.

AGNES. What astonishes me most—aside from my theoretically healthy fear—no, not fear, how silly of me—healthy speculation that I might some day become an embarrassment to you . . . what I find most astonishing in this world, and with all my years . . . is Claire.

TOBIAS *(curious)*. Claire? Why?

AGNES. That anyone—be they one's sister, or not—can be so . . . well, I don't want to use an unkind word, 'cause we're cozy here, aren't we?

TOBIAS *(smiled warning)*. Maybe.[8]

The progression of the scene might be described thus: a discussion of sanity and insanity is interrupted sporadically by a more pedestrian discussion of liqueurs only to return to a discussion of sanity and insanity. The physical progression that is forced by the lines is that Agnes and Tobias be apart and drinkless at the start and that they come together through the scene to be close and supplied with drinks at the end of the first build. The discussion of the relative merits of anisette and cognac are punctuations or accents through the first scene. We know they are accents because they are briefer, more prosaic, than the other lines. They are often even bounded by other prosaic and conventional lines. The short beat is a rhythmic device. Again some explanation of its use in drama may be inferred from an examination of its use in poetry. Suzanne Langer, in *Feeling and Form*, notes that the short or shorter beat is a device which, once discovered, was put to varied uses in poetry, some of which were its service "as a pause, as an accent, as an echo, as a closing chord, and undoubtedly a little research would reveal various other functions." All the uses mentioned seem to add up to two related effects: "to slow a rhythm" or "to halt it with a tone of finality."[9] Tobias's comments provide an interruption of Agnes's rhythm, and thus form an accent.

I do not mean to imply that because Claire is the first major accent and liqueurs provide minor accents that the play is either about Claire or liquor or alcoholism, even though Claire is an alcoholic. Albee has combined these accents with good reason, though, because his rhythmic devices continually point to half-conscious escape. Agnes cannot say, it seems, "What astonishes me most is Claire," without qualifying, explaining what the second most astonishing thing is. And she cannot explain the second most astonishing thing without qualification, intellectualization, rationalization. We could almost repunctuate Agnes's speech with parentheses, quite a lot of them. Albee calls for a pattern of escape, too, in the performance of Agnes's speech. It is written in such a way that the actress must constantly shift from outer-directed lines (contact with Tobias) to inner-directed lines (introspective escape). What is changing in this scene, then, is the nature of escape. There are several methods and means: digressions, introspection, drink, the pedestrian comments of daily life. And yet the change is ordered and consistent. There is a constant return to the discussion of the delicate balance between sanity, defined by implication as coping, and insanity, defined by Agnes and by the progression as escape or drifting.

We might state what actually happens in terms of a progression as follows: an issue is almost broached (Claire) but Agnes escapes. Tobias helps Agnes, probably for selfish reasons, to escape from her escape. The second escape (liqueurs) is a reminder of the unbroached issue, so Agnes escapes again. Being a tidy person, she traces her way back to the beginning and comes face to face with Tobias, the drinks, and the unbroached issue. By the time the issue is faced, we have become accustomed to the patterns of escape. The argument that Agnes and Tobias have is punctuated by changes of subject, driftings, philosophies, anything that will relieve the tedium of fighting a fight that can have no resolution. When Claire enters the room, Agnes escapes by leaving. Rhythmic dialogue lured us into the world of the play and prepared us by its repetitions for more of the same.

Albee tends to overlap the pattern throughout the play, much as he does in the first scene. Probably an audience if snapped to awareness at many points in the play would wonder how the characters got off the track but would feel fairly secure in guessing that they would eventually get back on if only because all tracks eventually lead home. Claire, angry with Agnes, says, "Agnes; why don't you die?" Tobias talks about Julia; Agnes and Tobias talk about conflict in love; then Agnes asks, "Do you really want me dead, Claire?" Claire's reply is a hopeless answer, but accurately thematic: "Wish, yes. Want? I don't know; probably, though I might regret it if I had it" (p. 42). In this play nothing can really be resolved. People can only verbalize what they have left unverbalized, usually proving that things are really as bad, maybe worse, than everyone thought. Since the talk of Agnes's death is unpleasant, Tobias interrupts with a recollection of an incident from his past. In a long (four-page) explanation, Tobias tells how he wished to kill his cat when it ceased to love him. Instead, he "had it killed." Incredibly similar to the story of Jerry and the dog from *The Zoo Story*, the cat story is a story of failure. If Tobias failed to get the cat to respond with love, he failed in a larger sense, and failure requires the snuffing out of the symbol of failure. Is the cat story a conscious or unconscious escape from the unpleasantness in the living room? Or is it a little of both? In any case it provides no real escape, but only a return to the issues at hand. The conclusion of the story implies its "moral," which is, as Albee might have phrased it, "We kill those we love when they do not love us back."

If the rhythm points to escape, what about Harry and Edna, escapers supreme. They leave their home because some formless terror seizes them when they are there alone. Their stay at the home of Agnes and Tobias does not resolve anything. It is hardly pleasant. And it confirms their worst fears—that they are alone, that they are not wanted, that they must return to what they fear. Agnes, Tobias, Julia, and Claire all escape often in their various ways only to come back to each other, which, one suspects, is what they were escaping from to begin with. Tobias, in one sense, left Agnes ages ago, retreated to his "own room," but he is faced with her silent reproaches daily.

The rhythmic repetitions in Albee's opening dialogue prepare us for the world of the play. That first progression—a long build which ends where it began—is mirrored in the action of the rest of the play. The patterns make the world of the play sound and look a little out of kilter. The style, not far from realism, yet not *quite* realism because of the odd manner of speaking which persists throughout the play, is, like the rhythm, part of the play's meaning.

Word repetition is a device which is appropriate in the contemporary drama. Modern ironic plays rely on patterning to make their ironic points in a drama which is not moving fast and may be moving very little indeed. Repetitions seem to hold the action and lower the spectators' level of expectancy of change. Martin Esslin, who finds the contemporary drama plotless and static (not in the naive sense of that observation), explains that the dramatist of the Theatre of the Absurd is concerned with presenting a poetic image over time.[10] An extreme absurdist like Ionesco repeats words to such an extent that he empties them of meaning. He creates a sense of ritualistic nonsense. But the sense of ritual, even in semiabsurdists like Pinter and Albee, is fostered by the repetition of semisensible words.

One of the roots of Absurdism, according to Esslin, is the tradition of nursery rhymes and nonsense verses. "We can be sure that nonsense rhymes have been sung to children and chanted by adults since the earliest times. There is a magic about nonsense, and magic formulas often consist of syllables that still have rhyme or rhythm but have lost any sense they may originally have contained."[11] Andrew Welsh, in a dissertation entitled "Melos and Opsis," investigates the roots of rhythm in poetry. In discussing what he calls "charm rhythm" (based on Frye's passage in *The Anatomy of Criticism*, quoted above), he deals with a rhythm based on the repetition of words. In many primitive charms verbal formula goes hand in hand with ritual action. Welsh finds, too, that "the repeated sound is more important than the meaning of any individual word." The primitive poems or charms which he cites were sung or chanted by their people. Primitive rituals were used to cause some other action.[12]

Investigations into the roots of verbal rhythm are interesting with regard to the ritualistic nature of contemporary drama, even when the ritual is married to realism, as it is in *A Delicate Balance*. The ritualistic rhythm of *A Slight Ache* is far more evident. Perhaps the most complex combination of sound rhythms, ritual, nonsense, and sense can be found in Beckett's *Waiting for Godot*. In this symmetrical and patterned play, Beckett uses word repetitions as only a poet can. The result of his openly rhythmic word play is a prose-poetry in which repetitions, changes, and progressions of any section in the play contribute to the complex poetry of the whole. Here is an interesting passage early in act 1 in which several kinds of word rhythm are used at once. The first seven lines, a unit in itself, utilizes a repetition of "It's" to start five of the lines, but this repetition only points to a more interesting rhythm, one based on reversal and synonymity. Estragon and Vladimir are examining Lucky. Their attention is first drawn to his neck:

ESTRAGON. Oh I say!
VLADIMIR. A running sore!
ESTRAGON. It's the rope.

VLADIMIR. It's the rubbing.
ESTRAGON. It's inevitable.
VLADIMIR. It's the knot.
ESTRAGON. It's the chafing. (P. 17)

Both tramps start with an exclamation. In addition to the sound-alike beginnings of lines with "It's," the words "running," "rope," and "rubbing" are also sound-alikes. "Rope" and "rubbing" are relatively synonymous with "knot" and "chafing," so that the tramps are really repeating themselves. These few lines, typical of many exchanges between Vladimir and Estragon, act as a microcosmic part of the whole play. The progression reminds us, perhaps subconsciously, of the progression of the entire work: distanced observations-interruption-observations, seemingly different from the first, but in fact only a bleaker paraphrase. The end result is sameness. Estragon and Vladimir exchange roles temporarily, this time with nouns and verbs. The remainder of this scene uses repetitions of "It's inevitable" in which the speakers take turns. "It's not certain" is also a recurring line which the speakers alternate. "Slobber" is connected with its sound-alike and mean-alike, "slaver." "Halfwit" is repeated in a synonym, "cretin." Through the whole passage the interdependence of Vladimir and Estragon is emphasized, and their dual observation, "It's inevitable," is a recurring accent because it occurs at approximately the same central spot in each minor progression.

(They resume their inspection, dwell on the face.)
VLADIMIR *(grudgingly)*. He's not bad looking.
ESTRAGON *(shrugging his shoulders, wry face)*. Would you say so?
VLADIMIR. A trifle effeminate.
ESTRAGON. Look at the slobber.
VLADIMIR. It's inevitable.
ESTRAGON. Look at the slaver.
VLADIMIR. Perhaps he's a halfwit.
ESTRAGON. A cretin.
VLADIMIR *(looking closer)*. Looks like a goiter.
ESTRAGON *(ditto)*. It's not certain.

VLADIMIR. He's panting.
ESTRAGON. It's inevitable.
VLADIMIR. And his eyes!
ESTRAGON. What about them?
VLADIMIR. Goggling out of his head.
ESTRAGON. Looks at his last gasp to me.
VLADIMIR. It's not certain. *(Pause.)* Ask him a question.   (Pp. 17–18)

Through all interruptions or changes in *Waiting for Godot,* the tramps end with repetition and sameness. In act 2, when Vladimir and Estragon cannot agree on anything, they decide self-consciously to talk calmly. They choose as their subject "all the dead voices." In this passage, as in many others, the alternation between speakers is so regular, the subject so tightly bounded, that Beckett again emphasizes the combined perception of life that characterizes the tramps' existence. Like Pozzo and Lucky, they are separate creatures (Vladimir who thinks, Estragon who reacts) and parts of the same creature (almost disillusioned humanity). Vladimir gives us a poetic vision of change in this passage, albeit consistent change, while Estragon provides us with consistency. As Esslin notes, "in what is probably the most lyrical, most perfectly phrased passage of the play . . . the cross-talk of Irish music-hall comedians is miraculously transmuted into poetry."[13]

ESTRAGON. All the dead voices.
VLADIMIR. They make a noise like wings.
ESTRAGON. Like leaves.
VLADIMIR. Like sand.
ESTRAGON. Like leaves.
    (Silence.)
VLADIMIR. They all speak at once.
ESTRAGON. Each one to itself.
    (Silence.)
VLADIMIR. Rather they whisper.
ESTRAGON. They rustle.
VLADIMIR. They murmur.
ESTRAGON. They rustle.
    (Silence.)

VLADIMIR. What do they say?
ESTRAGON. They talk about their lives.
VLADIMIR. To have lived is not enough for them.
ESTRAGON. They have to talk about it.
VLADIMIR. To be dead is not enough for them.
ESTRAGON. It is not sufficient.
   (Silence.)
VLADIMIR. They make a noise like feathers.
ESTRAGON. Like leaves.
VLADIMIR. Like ashes.
ESTRAGON. Like leaves.
   (Long silence.)
VLADIMIR. Say something!   (P. 40)

Günther Müller, in an essay called "Morphological Poetics," explains one of the sources of rhythm through sound. "Language does not merely form immaterial and incorporeal meanings but a 'tonal body' of varying sensuous power. It forms this tonal body by means of an articulated succession of bright and dark, low and high, broad and narrow tones and noises, and the articulated succession produces rhythm." Since sound creates meaning, meanings "grow" from the "tonal body" and are colored by it.[14]

Beckett achieves part of his rhythmic effect through a succession of bright and dark meanings based upon high and low tones. Vladimir's alternations are regular and consistent. He constantly moves from light images (the words even give us a lift) to heavy images. The combinations of key words in each section are: wings–sand, whisper–murmur, lived–dead, feathers–ashes. Estragon's repetitions set off these changes. The passage functions in several important ways. First of all it bears out the pattern of changes or interruptions giving way to sameness. Vladimir's changes always give way to Estragon's repetitions. The pauses always frame a new observation and give way eventually to the repeated pattern of four lines—Vladimir's changing, Estragon's not. The major interruption, in which the rhythms are more jagged, gives way to the passage most similar to the first: Estragon repeats "Like leaves." And, as if Beckett had not already made his horrifying point, the whole exercise in conversing ends in anguished recognition that the conversation didn't work. It was simply another change after which nothing is changed.

The "insulting" scene later in the act is worth looking at for an interesting variation on comic rhythm. Interruption is again a factor: this time the insults are interrupted by a partial recognition of the pleasure derived from hurling insults. The result of that recognition is that Vladimir and Estragon continue to call each other names, but now in a self-conscious manner. It seems almost as if the sound of one insulting word provides the idea for the next word or phrase. In the tradition of nonsense verse, the words are empty of meaning but they are not empty of sound. As a matter of fact, much of the rhythm is dependent upon sound cognates and the rearrangement of single sounds. As Kenneth Burke points out in his essay, "On Musicality in Verse," often when we feel a series of words is related, but we do not know why, probably similar or cognate sounds are at work. *B*, *m*, and *p*, for instance, are close phonetic relatives. A writer can and often does juggle sounds much like a composer does melodies, playing them backward or upside down so that they are different, but closely related.[15] Such juggling of sounds in playwriting is just another illustration of the principle of repetition and change at work. The end of the "insulting" scene is particularly interesting in terms of repeated sounds.

VLADIMIR. Ceremonious ape!
ESTRAGON. Punctilious pig!
VLADIMIR. Finish your phrase, I tell you!
ESTRAGON. Finish your own!
 (Silence. They draw closer, halt.)
VLADIMIR. Moron!
ESTRAGON. That's the idea, let's abuse each other.
 (They turn, move apart, turn again and face each other.)
VLADIMIR. Moron!
ESTRAGON. Vermin!
VLADIMIR. Abortion!
ESTRAGON. Morpion!

VLADIMIR. Sewer-rat!
ESTRAGON. Curate!
VLADIMIR. Cretin!
ESTRAGON *(with finality)*. Crritic!
VLADIMIR. Oh! (P. 48)

In another well-known exchange from act 2, Vladimir and Estragon discuss "exercising." The rhythm is supported by parallel beginnings of sentences. It is also supported by Estragon's
repetitions. As usual Vladimir speaks the changes. Yet change
is consistent because "exercises," "elevations," and "elongations," are not only sound-alikes, but are related in meaning.
The last two, especially, imply expansion. As Vladimir's words
continue to suggest action and change, Estragon's suggest passivity and sameness. The rhythm is resolved, appropriately,
with Vladimir's "up," and Estragon's "down."

VLADIMIR. We could do our exercises.
ESTRAGON. Our movements.
VLADIMIR. Our elevations.
ESTRAGON. Our relaxations.
VLADIMIR. Our elongations.
ESTRAGON. Our relaxations.
VLADIMIR. To warm us up.
ESTRAGON. To calm us down.
VLADIMIR. Off we go. (P. 49)

If Beckett is a poet, he is nowhere a finer one than in Pozzo's
speech about blindness (act 2), which is poetry at its most complex in this play. Beckett again relies upon the rhythm of word
repetitions to sum up the philosophy of the play in a brief second. The speech calls attention to itself; it tells us that it is
poetry by its repetition. But that repetition is far from simple in
meaning.

POZZO *(suddenly furious)*. Have you not done tormenting me with your
accursed time! It's abominable! When! When! One day, is that not
enough for you, one day he went dumb, one day I went blind, one day
we'll go deaf, one day we were born, one day we shall die, the same
day, the same second, is that not enough for you? *(Calmer.)* They give

birth astride of a grave, the light gleams an instant, then it's night once more. *(He jerks the rope.)* On! (P. 57)

Words like "one" and "we" take on universal meaning. "One day we were born, one day we shall die, the same day, the same second" suggests (1) that everyone who has been born will die, (2) that Pozzo and Lucky will die, (3) that Pozzo and Lucky will die on the same day, for they are bound to each other, and (4) a lifetime is a day, a second—birth and death take place on the same day. "The light gleams an instant" means at one and the same time that life is only a brief second long, that illumination or recognition is brief and fleeting, and that we are all blanked out by a death in life, in which we become dumb, blind, and deaf to what we cannot bear. When rhythmic dialogue is used poetically in a play, as it is in *Waiting for Godot,* it can stop the action for a moment to make us understand ultimate meanings by holding our attention on words that are juxtaposed and combined complexly.

Modern dramatists, by using sound repetitions, often achieve a combined sense of the nursery rhyme and the ritual chant in their works. Suppose, however, a playwright neither opens his play with rhythmic sound repetitions nor ever uses them to the degree that Pinter, Albee, and Beckett have in the above examples; yet at some point in the play, a rhythmic repetition emerges obviously, too obviously to be ignored. Is there any similarity of effect or any consistency of response from the audience to this particular manifestation of rhythm? There appears to be, to some degree at least. Characters are often moved to use evident rhythms or rhetorically repetitive speech when words are all that is left, when action is impossible, or not worth the effort, or useless. Ironically, in instances like these, the words themselves generally prove inadequate. Rhythm pronounced somewhere in mid play, then, may have an effect not wholly different from rhythm pronounced at the opening of a play. The difference is one of degree. What we understand as useless is a particular action, not the action of the whole play. The heavily rhythmic passage functions as a "minor form" in

Burke's terminology. In other words, the speech (and it is more likely to be one speech than a dialogue between two or more characters) is a self-contained unit.

When Troilus witnesses Cressida's infidelity and can do nothing about it, he resorts to words, inadequate though they are, to solve the situation. Troilus, of course, does not direct the words *to* Cressida. He can find comfort only in patterning words and in beating Cressida through the pattern. The blank verse, an especially flexible and complex meter, is a great organizer of this speech. But so is Shakespeare's rhetorical word repetition:

TROILUS. This she? No, this is Diomed's Cressida.
   If beauty have a soul, this is not she;
   If souls guide vows, if vows be sanctimonies,
   If sanctimony be the gods' delight;
   If there be rule in unity itself,
   This is not she. O madness of discourse,
   That cause sets up with and against itself!
   Bi-fold authority, where reason can revolt
   Without perdition, and loss assume all reason
   Without revolt. This is, and is not, Cressid.
   Within my soul there doth conduce a fight
   Of this strange nature, that a thing inseparate
   Divides more wider than the sky and earth;
   And yet the spacious breadth of this division
   Admits no orifex for a point as subtle
   As Ariachne's broken woof to enter.
   Instance, o instance, strong as Pluto's gates;
   Cressid is mine, tied with the bonds of heaven.
   Instance, o instance, strong as heaven itself;
   The bonds of heaven are slipped, dissolved, and loosed;
   And with another knot, five-finger-tied,
   The fractions of her faith, orts of her love,
   The fragments, scraps, the bits, and greasy relics
   Of her o'er-eaten faith, are bound to Diomed.   (5.2.137–60)

When Horatio cannot physically stay the Ghost, he resorts to a rhythmic supplication. This speech builds in frustration as Horatio crams more and more elements of persuasion between his pleas. He appears to be trying to prove to the Ghost that he, Horatio, is worthy of hearing. Repetition occurs as a short beat, and in addition to the word repetition ("Stay" and "Speak") is a repetition in "timing." The short beat, as Langer points out, can slow or halt a progression. In this case, it slows the tumbling words of Horatio.

> But soft, behold, lo where it comes again.
> I'll cross it, though it blast me. Stay illusion,
> If thou hast any sound or use of voice,
> Speak to me.
> If there be any good thing to be done
> That may to thee do ease, and grace to me,
> Speak to me.
> If thou art privy to thy country's fate
> Which happily foreknowing may avoid,
> O speak.
> Or if thou hast uphoarded in thy life
> Extorted treasure in the womb of earth,
> For which they say you spirits oft walk in death,
> Speak of it; stay and speak. Stop it Marcellus.   (Ham. 1.1.126–39)

When Hamlet feels that he can no longer attempt to control or change the course of events or even to understand the logic of the universe, he uses rhythmic prose to say, in effect, "nothing to be done":

> If it be now, 'tis not to come; if it be not to come, it will be now; if it be not now, yet it will come—the readiness is all. Since no man of aught he leaves knows, what is't to leave betimes? Let be.   (5.2.231–35)

This speech of Hamlet's has a much calmer effect than either Troilus' or Horatio's because it is so symmetrically balanced with its triple emphasis on "come" and "now." We hear almost a prayer for death: now come, come now, now come. The rhythm is a strangely lulling one.

Perhaps since rhetorical speech calls attention to itself, it makes us especially aware of whether or not it is accomplishing anything. Are the words used as words, flung to the empty air?

Or do they, laden with meaning, hit a target? They are more likely to hit a target in plays where verbal grandeur is in order. The third act of *Julius Caesar* is a case in point. In this play, which is as much about persuasion as about anything else, words are extremely important and effective. It is not that Brutus' rhetoric does not work. It is that Antony's more bombastic rhetoric works better. The rhythm of Antony's speech is organized by the repetitions through slightly varied paraphrases of two lines: "But Brutus says, he was ambitious, / And Brutus is an honourable man" (3.2.91–92).

It is no surprise to find rhetorical repetition providing the organizing rhythm of particular scenes or speeches in modern surrealistic or absurdist dramas or, for that matter, in Shakespeare or other Elizabethans. In both styles there is often an open investigation of and a toying with language. Both styles can afford a formalization of language. We tend not to find open word repetition in a "naturalistic" play, but when we do, the effects are somewhat different from other styles. The repetition must be motivated somehow. Vanya, in act 1 of Chekhov's *Uncle Vanya*, uses rhythmic repetition to phrase his frustration with the professor. He uses it on purpose to make a point about Serebryakov's uselessness:

> The man has been lecturing and writing about art for twenty-five years, though he knows absolutely nothing about art. For twenty-five years he has been chewing over other men's ideas about realism, naturalism, and all sorts of nonsense; for twenty-five years he has been lecturing and writing about things all intelligent people know about already and stupid ones aren't interested in—so for twenty-five years he has been simply wasting his time. And with all that, what conceit! What pretensions! He has retired, and not a living soul knows anything about him; he is absolutely unknown. So that for twenty-five years all he has done is to keep a better man out of a job! But just look at him: he struts about like a demi-god! (P. 197)

The repetition of "twenty-five years" makes the speech rhetorical, but it is the rhetoric of frustration. As a rhythmic organizer of the thoughts, the phrase points up Vanya's concern with wasted time. In addition, the repetitions frame Vanya's explosions which generally have to do with the professor's egomania. The important thing is, though, that all Vanya *can* do is repeat himself. The speech illustrates not only the rhetoric of frustration, but the rhythm of frustration. The progression or overall pattern of repetitions and changes in this speech is not unlike the overall pattern of the entire play. A theme is repeated with variations. The climax never quite hits a climactic point, partly because of timing: it is overstated, drawn-out. If Vanya had ended with "wasting his time," he might have spoken a rather tight bit of rhetoric. But instead, he goes on to repeat himself in anticlimax and even manages to draw out the anticlimax.

Also from *Uncle Vanya* is the following rather complex example of rhythmic effect that occurs at the end of the play. Here no character is consciously or willfully creating a pattern. Serebryakov and Yelena have just left by carriage. Astrov and Vanya are alone in the room. Marina and Sonya enter separately, each repeating Astrov's observation that the professor and his wife are gone. Neither entering character is aware of repeating. Finally Marya enters, rounding out the pattern:

> *(A pause; there is the sound of bells.)*
> ASTROV. They've gone. The Professor is glad, I'll be bound. Nothing will tempt him back.
> MARINA *(enters)*. They've gone *(sits down in an easy chair and knits her stocking)*.
> SONYA *(enters)*. They've gone *(wipes her eyes)*. Good luck to them. *(To her uncle)* Well, Uncle Vanya, let us do something.
> VOYNITSKY. Work, work. . . .
> SONYA. It's ever so long since we sat at this table together *(lights the lamp on the table)*. I believe there is no ink *(takes the inkstand, goes to the cupboard, and fills it with ink)*. But I feel sad that they have gone.
> *(MARYA VASSILYEVNA comes in slowly.)*
> MARYA. They've gone *(sits down and becomes engrossed in reading)*.
> (P. 241)

"They've gone" is repeated five times, just as "twenty-five years" was. And yet each line is capable of very specific motivation. Astrov says it to fill a deadly pause; he is simply saying the obvious. Marina, as usual, lets everything that goes into her head come out her mouth. She is a somewhat oblivious news-reporter. Since she was not at all happy with the Professor's visit, she may even be a little relieved. Sonya reacts emotionally, shows her emotions, fights them, shows them again. The line takes on a different character when Sonya speaks. Marya may even be a little reproachful when she enters, repeating "They've gone," for she was on the Professor's side, and she restates her position by becoming engrossed in reading upon her entrance.

Chekhov has placed us once more on that thin borderline between pathos and comedy. We are painfully aware of what is unsaid, what the departure means to Astrov, Vanya, and Sonya. We are aware, too, that no words are really more adequate than the simple "They've gone." However, the words are spoken not only by those who have lost a great deal, but by those who have lost nothing. Four characters unconsciously creating a pattern are apt to be comic. Indeed it is Chekhov's particular method of ironic comedy to show us a pattern in which the characters are unconscious participants and in which, as a matter of fact, those characters *believe* they are behaving in an independent human way. Chekhov shows his audience the extent to which the characters are merely puppets. The comedy here is by no means laughing comedy. It is the sort of comedy that persistently emerges from our tears.

An interesting thing about the rhythm of the scene, however, is the pattern of repetition, painfully long climax, and anticlimax. The first three instances of "They've gone" provide in addition to those words an elaboration of the comment, either verbal or physical, each elaboration taking approximately equal time. But the choral ode does not end with "Good luck to them." Instead, what seems like an interruption—getting to work—is really a continuation of the climax, so that its refusal to resolve itself is painful. The repetition is an echo: "But I feel sad that they have gone." The dull climax resolves itself in anticlimax,

as Marya, the least sympathetic character of the piece, and one
we have probably forgotten about, finishes the ode.

If the chorus on the departure of Serebryakov and Yelena is
pathetic, laced with comedy, and a reminder through regularly
rhythmic words that there is nothing to be said, nothing to be
done, what about the echo of that scene, not many moments later when Astrov has left as well? At the sound of bells, Marina
says, "He has gone." There is a pause. Sonya enters and, we
are told, puts the candle on the table. "He has gone" (p. 243). In
this brilliantly controlled rhythm, the pause, the action of
Sonya, and the simplicity of the two repetitions remind us of the
pathetic rather than the comic implications of the situation and
prepare us for the ironic repetitions of the final speech.

Chekhov uses openly rhythmic speech to end his *Uncle Vanya*
and *Three Sisters*. The speeches of each stand out because of
their rhythmic qualities. They point to irony as most patterned
words do. Sonya's speech is particularly interesting because of
the repeated words, repeated phrases, and repeated sentence
structures. Both builds of the monologue end in "We shall rest,"
each time repeated thrice. A triple repeat on "We shall rest,"
might have been calming—almost like Hamlet's "Come now"
speech. But Sonya repeats the line some six times, in two groupings of three, which gives the passage a sense of desperateness,
of protesting too much. In addition, Chekhov undercuts the progression by ironic interruptions of sound from Telyegin's guitar
and the Watchman's tapping, in addition to the visual irony of
Marina's knitting and Marya's note-taking. Telyegin's guitar is
supportive of Sonya's emotional outburst and an interruption of
her outburst at one and the same time. The Watchman's tap
represents security, ironic for those in a prison, yet a reminder
that daily life goes on in the present tense. And it is an interruption by one whom we never see, and who in the "realistic" sense
has no idea of what is being felt inside the window. In the symbolic sense, he is like a prison guard, making his rounds. Meanwhile Sonya and Vanya must look to the far future, to life after
death, for release from their sorrows.

VOYNITSKY *(to* SONYA, *passing his hand over her hair).* My child, how my
heart aches! Oh, if only you knew how my heart aches!

SONYA. There is nothing for it. We must go on living! *(a pause)* We shall
go on living, Uncle Vanya! We shall live through a long, long chain of
days and weary evenings; we shall patiently bear the trials which
fate sends us; we shall work for others, both now and in our old age,
and have no rest; and when our time comes we shall die without a
murmur, and there beyond the grave we shall say that we have suf-
fered, that we have wept, that life has been bitter to us, and God will
have pity on us, and you and I, uncle, dear uncle, shall see a life that
is bright, lovely, beautiful. We shall rejoice and look back at these
troubles of ours with tenderness, with a smile—and we shall rest. I
have faith, uncle; I have fervent, passionate faith. *(Slips on her knees
before him and lays her head on his hands; in a weary voice)* We shall
rest!

   *(*TELYEGIN *softly plays on the guitar.)*

SONYA. We shall rest! We shall hear the angels; we shall see all Heaven
lit with radiance; we shall see all earthly evil, all our sufferings
drowned in mercy which will fill the whole world, and our life will be
peaceful, gentle and sweet as a caress. I have faith, I have faith
(wipes away his tears with her handkerchief). Poor Uncle Vanya, you
are crying. *(Through her tears)* You have had no joy in your life, but
wait, Uncle Vanya, wait. We shall rest *(puts her arms around him).*
We shall rest! *(The Watchman taps.)*

   *(*TELYEGIN *plays softly;* MARYA VASSILYEVNA *makes notes on the
   margin of her pamphlet;* MARINA *knits her stocking.)*

SONYA. We shall rest! (Pp. 243–44)

This speech follows the pattern of climax and anticlimax in a
manner similar to the others quoted. Sonya has finished a "poetic" thought with the first triplet of "We shall rest." But she
goes on to embellish the thought only making it less climactic,
less definite. Vanya's and her tears betray them, making the
last series of "We shall rest" the final anticlimax.

Chekhov has the protagonists of *Three Sisters* verbalize the
rhythm of the play, much as Sonya does, in the final scene of the
play. Certainly there is some disservice to Chekhov in choosing
anything from his total pattern and considering it separate

from the other parts. It should be understood that the following exercise merely uncovers the skeleton of the final rhythm of *Three Sisters*. If we extract the repetitive dialogue and the ironic sound effects from the scene we can better see the bones of the scene. Tchebutykin's comments, too important to ignore, are included. He, too, repeats himself.

TCHEBUTYKIN. . . . "Tarara-boom-dee-ay" . . . It doesn't matter.

MASHA. Oh, listen to that band! . . . We've got to live . . . we've got to live. . . .

IRINA. . . . A time will come when everyone will know what all this is for. . . . we have got to live . . . we have got to work, only to work! . . . and I will work, I will work.

OLGA. . . . The music is so gay, so confident. . . . We shall live! The music is so gay, so joyful. . . . we shall know what we are living for. . . . If we only knew—if we only knew!

   (*The music grows more and more subdued.* . . .)

TCHEBUTYKIN. . . . "Tarara-boom-dee-ay!". . . . It doesn't matter, it doesn't matter.

OLGA. If we only knew, if we only knew!   (Pp. 188–89)

There are many double lines in many patterns so that we become accustomed to them: "to live, to live" and "to work, to work," prepare the way for the less enthusiastic pairs of phrases at the end of the progression. Olga's optimism and the faltering of it provide the long climax and its reversal to anticlimax which is typical of the major rhythmic sweep in all of Chekhov's plays. As almost every critic points out, we cannot afford to miss the fact that we are treated to an important visual irony in the tableau. Kuligin comes to fetch his Masha. Andrey is still wheeling the pram. This is the visual parallel to the fading of the music. Brustein describes the last scene as a playing out of "the dialectic of hope and despair in a situation of defeat."[16] Although David Magarshack finds the play's ending frankly hopeful, he has little company, at least among critics. John L. Styan sees no comfort in the overall pattern, but he does find some reassurance in the sensitivity of the three sisters, whose positive attitude is part of an overall cluster of impressions.[17]

Frye locates Chekhov in the extreme ironic phase of comedy. And he cites particularly the last act of *Three Sisters* as pure irony.[18] States concurs about both Chekhov and the final moments of *Three Sisters.* He sees the final chorus as a reminder that the sisters' souls have stirred with joy before, that once again a light melody is played against bitter reality, providing counterpoint: "the dream life, frail but persistent still, struggling in the coils of its reality, throwing against reality the only defense Chekhov has allowed it to possess, a refusal to face the awful truth."[19] Not only do the lines of hope at the end of the *Three Sisters* have to be repeated twice at least and the lines of resolution (work) have to be repeated even more often, but those lines frame others in which time is not standing still: "Now it's autumn; soon winter will come and cover us with snow" and "O my God! Time will pass, and we shall go away forever, and we shall be forgotten" (p. 188). The fact that the dialectic gives way to "if we only knew" repeated four times is some indication of how frail and how persistent hope and resolution have become.

Repeated words, here as in other examples of ironic plays or ironic moments in dramatic literature, call attention to themselves and pose questions. Where is the rhetoric directed? Does it work? In ironic plays, the words are just that, words. They become symbols in themselves, rather than symbols for things or ideas which can be better handled by skill at handling the words. They are not used *for* something; they are used *instead of* something.

In conclusion, repetition of sounds, words, and phrases in drama is a rhythmic device. The device often provides an obvious pulse in both verse and prose drama. Our pleasure and understanding do not end with the sense of pulse, however. The repetitions tend to point a finger at the departure from repetition and thus provide orderly and measurable changes which, as Boleslavsky notes, are clues to meaning. Repetitions and changes are the means of progression, and progression is a necessary factor in all art, but particularly in the temporal arts, music and drama. All dialogue repetitions are rhetorical to some extent, and as such they indicate the effectiveness or lack of effectiveness of words. We ask, is the chant nonsensical, empty, or persuasive?

Alternation of Speaker
and Length of Speech

To be sure, all dialogue is rhythmic. Boleslavsky says somewhat
facetiously that every stone in the universe has rhythm—a few
actors perhaps do not—but every stone *does*.[1] Somewhere
there may perhaps be dialogue without rhythm, but we are
fairly safe in assuming that dialogue is rhythmic in any adequate play and excitingly rhythmic in a great play. Repetition of
sounds, words, and phrases emphasizes rhythm and makes it
obvious. Other kinds of patterning in dialogue are not nearly so
obvious. We may assume that playwrights, by unconscious or
deliberate design, make some of their rhythms obvious while
others are subtler and less intrusive.

We know that if we are to have drama there must be more
than one speaker and there must be some exchange between
them. Through this exchange, no matter how minimal (Krapp
and his tape) or how varied (some thirty speaking characters in
Hamlet) one of the larger rhythmic patterns generally emerges.
It may be as subtle or as obvious as other kinds of rhythm. The
more evident, of course, the more the pattern calls attention to
itself as a pattern and creates an expectation for more of the
same. The conscious appreciation of pattern operates somewhat like Burke's "conventional form," which "involves to some
degree the appeal of form *as form*. . . . When a form appeals as
form, we designate it as conventional form. Any form can become conventional, and be sought for itself—whether it be as

complex as the Greek tragedy or as compact as the sonnet." An interesting phenomenon is that conventional form can create an appetite or an expectation *before* reading or observing the work of art.[2]

Let us consider two subjects in this section, since they are related: length of individual speeches and speaker alternation (or the pattern of exchanges). We tend to understand and perceive alternation by awareness of the length of speeches and length by awareness of alternation.

The first example that comes to mind is Burke's first example of conventional form: the typical pattern of Greek tragedy. A prologue—expository monologue or dialogue—generally begins the play. A song and dance by the chorus, known as the parodos, and generally performed as they enter, follows. Next comes a scene between characters or between character and chorus known as an episode. A choral ode or stasimon follows the episode. The remainder of the play is made up of an alternation between episodes and stasima until the final choral ode which is known as the exodos. The choral stasimon itself is divided into parts: strophe, antistrophe, and epode. There may be any number of alternating strophes and antistrophes—metrically identical stanzas—before the epode or concluding stanza is sung. Whether the whole chorus sang the whole stasimon or parts of the chorus sang parts of the stasimon, the fact remains that the chorus was a recurring speaker. And as a recurring speaker it brought to the play lyrical comment upon the action. The chorus served to distance the audience and to make the situation of the episodes magnificent or larger than life, universal, and important. Schiller explains well the function of the chorus:

It forsakes the contracted sphere of the incidents to dilate itself over the past and the future, over distant times and nations, and general humanity, to deduce the grand results of life, and pronounce the lessons of wisdom. But all this it does with the full power of fancy—with a bold lyrical freedom which ascends, as with godlike step, to the topmost height of worldly things; and it effects it in conjunction with the whole sensible influences of melody and rhythm, in tones and movements.[3]

Let us grant then that choral odes lend grandeur to the play as a whole. The fact that they alternate with episodes between characters is indicative of some sort of regular pattern of distancing and magnifying. The length of the choral odes is therefore important. Aeschylus, the most lyric of ancient tragedians, uses the chorus to fill one-half to three-fifths of his stage time.[4] The chorus is a major part of the fabric of his tragedy and lends its tone to the whole. Sophocles uses the chorus a little less, probably for something less than half of his stage time. The result is that the chorus is supportive to and secondary to the heroes. Of course, other factors—the materials of the odes, for example— are important as well. But stage time should not be minimized. Richmond Lattimore explains the differences between Aeschylus and Sophocles in the following terms: the Trojan war is really the subject of the *Agamemnon*, but although the Theban war is important to the plot of *Antigone*, the play is not about that war. "In Sophocles, the choruses are commentaries on the action, not part of the larger action, and their imagery is functional to the choruses themselves but not to the tragedy as a whole."[5]

Since the use of the chorus diminished considerably in Euripides' hands, the focus of the drama (more time spent on episodes) forces the playwright and the spectator to concentrate even more on character and allows Euripides to develop character in a more realistic or psychological sense. No one disputes the fact that Euripides' characters are generally far less grand than those of either Aeschylus or Sophocles.

Where does this lead us? It is not an unreasonable assumption that the whole takes on the characteristics of its parts in some proportion to the emphasis each of the parts receives. But is this a manifestation of rhythm? It is certainly an orderly and measurable change of focus in a Greek tragedy. One could beat out on a set of drums the relationship between the characters and chorus. The regular recurrence of the chorus can provide a sense of stability to the rhythm of the whole. It may also, as a stabilizing factor, point the way to bigger changes or progressions. For instance, the chorus in *Oedipus* early in the play sings a lament about Thebes. Later in the play, their songs are about Oedipus and his fate. Their change of focus is a progression and provides a comment on the progression of the play as a whole.

The Greek tragic poets patterned episodes between character and character as well as between character and chorus to tell the story. In the first major confrontation of the play, Oedipus controls the scene with Teiresias not only by his confidence but by his wealth of words when he greets the prophet. After a pattern of fairly regular exchanges in which Oedipus provokes Teiresias to tell the truth, Oedipus answers with long and eloquent rage. After a brief interruption from the chorus, the stage belongs to Teiresias. In a speech matching in length almost identically the most recent explosion of Oedipus (in the David Grene translation), Teiresias defends himself by giving further particulars of the curse. After a far briefer section of relatively equal exchanges between the two men, a long speech of prediction by the old prophet finishes the episode. The speech is approximately as long as Oedipus' first speech of greeting.[6] The episode itself is symmetrical in pattern, but for the brief moment of equality between the opponents in the second half. The change is part of the progression of the scene. Also part of the progression is the reversal—simply in the power of stage time—between Oedipus and Teiresias. Rhythm—repetition, change, and progression—can exist on a temporal level, perhaps unnoticed by the audience intellectually, but certainly noticed emotionally. That temporal level is the length and pattern of speaker alternation.

Length of speeches, as well as the alternation pattern between speakers is a key to the dialogue rhythm of an entire play. In some cases, silly though it may sound, a sense of overall dialogue rhythm can be gleaned by simply skimming through the pages of a clearly printed text. For instance, fifteen seconds with the printed pages of Beckett's *Happy Days* is sufficient to tell a skimmer who is unfamiliar with the play that Winnie's changes have a great deal to do with Willie, that Willie is terribly important, and that he hardly exists.

A cursory examination of *Waiting for Godot* tells us the following facts about the overall dialogue rhythm. Vladimir and Estragon speak primarily in one-liners, the exception being Vladimir's occasional forays into slightly extended thought, Estragon's occasional prolonged joking or wheedling. No speech extends much past five or six lines. Pozzo enters. He has several extended speeches, and in his presence Vladimir and Estragon resort to one-liners. Lucky, of course, has a single, very long speech. Pozzo takes his exit in act 1 with a much interrupted monologue of gathering himself, his things, his Lucky, and his words as he says farewell. We are back to Vladimir's and Estragon's one-liners and the Boy's half-liners. Act 2, in many ways a mirror of act 1, has some important differences. Vladimir's speeches get increasingly longer. Estragon's do not. (In fact he sleeps more, engages in conversation less.) Pozzo, "the speaker," has only one extended speech, and Lucky, now dumb, has none. Otherwise Didi and Gogo still have moments of relatively equal exchanges, and the Boy continues with his half-liners. There is patterning here, certainly. There is, as a result, rhythmic progression. But does it provide anything more than a pleasantly accurate pulse? If so, the progression should mean something and should make us feel something as well.

Beckett provides a kind of equilibrium before Pozzo's act 1 entrance. The tramps keep up a comic banter, comic in the "music-hall style." This atmosphere of regularity in despair is broken or interrupted by the entrance of master and slave. Pozzo takes the stage from the tramps, and they become a kind of ironic chorus to his bombastic (tragical, philosophical-heroical) rhetoric. Pozzo's rhetoric is fragile. He learned to think and speak from Lucky, he tells the tramps, but it appears he loses his place and his words much of the time. He is, to say the least, self-conscious. When Lucky speaks, with more absurdity and nonsense than anyone has previously, we get a hint of great sense buried somewhere deep beneath the nonsense. At least half the sense or half the irony is expressed in these few words, much interrupted by qualifications (which are not so clear): "Given the existence . . . of a personal God . . . who . . . loves us dearly with some exceptions." The other half of the sense comes from bitterly comic images of a white beard, divine apathy, and divine aphasia, as well as the recurrent "for reasons unknown" (act 1, p. 28). Lucky wears out the hysterical potential of speech in this play. Nothing from this point on will be quite so wild. Yet this speech clues us in to something important. Beneath nonsense is sense, but sense amounts to the bitter truth of senselessness. The labors of man are guesses or hypotheses or attempts, all of which exist concurrently, simultaneously, for reasons unknown. God, if he exists, is aphasic, but so is everyone else in this play in a metaphoric sense. Lucky is at the very center of the play. His silence, broken once, is important. Lucky's knowledge is too much and Pozzo's words have been too much. When they leave the stage, they leave the tramps to return to a brief interlude of bearable misery only to be faced with the Boy, a perfect rhythmic balance to Pozzo and Lucky. Neither his knowledge nor his words are enough.

Act 2 provides the stability of sameness (a precarious equilibrium between the tramps, another entrance by Pozzo and Lucky, another message from the Boy) but with important variations. Expression is perhaps a constant quantity like tears. Vladimir and Estragon are both more nonsensical (the "insulting" scene) and more lyrical (the "dead voices" scene.) Lucky speaks no more. Pozzo speaks far less, but now the "blind" speech, a parallel to the bombastic "night" speech, is far more lyrical, more profound, more emotional than his act 1 speech. It takes far fewer words to say what he has to say. Vladimir, now the possessor of Lucky's hat, philosophizes more. And finally, there are no really long speeches in act 2, which, in terms of rhythm, as well as of symbolic extension, is a great equalizer. As in all rhythmic manifestations, something remains stable, something else changes, there is a progression leading to the final aim of the artist.

Even in a play with as many characters and scenes as *Hamlet,* there appears to be a discernible rhythm of alternation between speakers and of the length of speeches. Although the play has some share of speeches of moderate length (ten to twenty lines), it has a preponderance of exchanges made up of short speeches (one to three lines per speaker) balanced by very long speeches, including the soliloquies (thirty lines or more). If we apply the old rule of thumb that most short speeches move the play quickly when they are patterned into exchanges and most long speeches slow down the action, we may conclude that the overall rhythm of the dialogue in *Hamlet* is irregular rather than regular, that it possesses emotional stops and starts. Is there any meaning to be attached to the recurring irregularity? Horatio, certainly a focal character in the first scene, second only to the Ghost in importance, is quite scanty of speech early in the scene. He answers questions and makes comments not only briefly, but with a hint of the special investigator who does not reveal too much. "Friends to this ground," substitutes for his and Marcellus' names. "A piece of him," is both more and less of an answer than was expected or needed to "What, is Horatio there?" Considering he is the guest of honor in the late night vigil, he warms up slowly, guarding his privacy for some time. "Tush, tush, 'twill not appear." He is supposed to be fortified against the story and we might well believe it. "Well, sit we down, / And let us hear Barnardo speak of this" (1.1.15–36). His brevity almost teases us to pay attention when he volunteers the expository information of the play, the story of the elder Hamlet's combat with Fortinbras and its attendant bad feelings. It is a speech of nearly thirty lines and it is glaringly long. If this were the only time Shakespeare had used the pattern of especially brief speech giving way to especially lengthy speech, we might chalk it up simply as a clever way to focus attention on part of the exposition.

In the second scene, Hamlet is the hidden focal character, Claudius the obvious one. After a long silence, Hamlet answers Claudius only when addressed, and then in quite brief riddles and puns. "A little more than kin, and less than kind" and "Not so my lord, I am too much in the sun." Even his "Seems, Madam?" speech (1.2.65–86) is rather grudging. This is not to say he is grudging of ideas, for as States points out, he lists in series what does *not* denote him truly.[7] But he is grudging of free expression which would bind him to Claudius and Gertrude emotionally. We are therefore prepared to listen when his relative silence is balanced by glorious expression in the thirty-line soliloquy which begins "O that this too too solid flesh would melt" (1.2.129).

The Ghost, too, over several scenes teases us and horrifies the guardsmen with his silence. And as if we were not already prepared to listen, "Mark me" is followed by hints and partial answers before the full story of the former king's murder is unraveled. When he finally does speak, States points out with some amusement, he is anything but brief. He may say, "Brief let me be," but "that great talker" treats Hamlet to "two anatomizations of the body in a state of seizure."[8] The dumb show (a broad hint, granted, but a silent one) precedes the play within the play. And cutting across scenic divisions, Claudius teases us with a hint as to the workings of his conscience in act 3, scene 1: "How smart a lash that speech doth give my conscience. / . . . O heavy burden! (50, 54). We get the full expression of that internal conflict two scenes later with "O, my offence is rank" (3.3.36).

Of the many dialogue rhythms that unite Shakespeare's *Hamlet,* the brief or scanty reply followed by, and balanced by, a long release of information or emotion tells us a great deal about the progression and the meaning of the play. A sense of intrigue is the product of this rhythmic progression and the rhythm itself is one of delay. What remains consistent in each separate case is restraint of some knowledge or emotion via verbal restraint. Change occurs when restraint gives way to expression, and when it does, information and emotion flow like a dam released.

In a sense, one of the issues in speaker patterns is silence. When we are not dealing with silence per se, we are often dealing, as in *Hamlet,* with relative silence. Gisèle Brelet in an essay, "Music and Silence," makes some interesting comments upon the functions of silence (and music and drama are much alike in their uses of silence). To Brelet, silence both precedes and follows music as well as surrounds it. Since silence envelops music, it provides the space or freedom which music will eventually order. And it "sets off" sound. "Silence is thus the symbol of possibility—and of freedom; furnisher of possibilities. . . . If sound seems to surge forth from silence, it is because it cannot in fact be born except from the movement by which, in silence, activity was already orienting itself towards the making of sound."[9]

Brelet distinguishes between two types of silence, but the categorization is not precisely the same as Pinter's. Brelet's two kinds of silence are "that which must remain empty, and that which must be filled." A silence that intervenes between melodies which have already been expressed is an empty one, precisely because its function is to separate "in order that the melody which is dying away may come to an end and close in upon itself."[10] Empty silence seems to describe well the pauses in *A Slight Ache.* Those silences constantly separate Edward and Flora, just as the Matchseller, one enormous representation of a pause, separates them. The pauses ask us to expect more of the same, but they also say, in effect, that some melody is dying out.

The second type of silence is, of course, the silence of expectation. It describes many silent or "quiet" characters in drama. Horatio of the first scene in *Hamlet,* Hamlet of the second scene, the Masha of *Three Sisters,* Lucky of *Waiting for Godot,* Willie of *Happy Days,* and all their fellows play out the silence of expectation. Their very silence at the opening of their respective scenes promises us music. Eventually that silence is balanced by sound, and we are reminded of one of two lessons we learned long ago, either that still waters run deep or that silence is indeed empty. To Brelet, in music, the alternation between silence and sound is rhythm. The same principle applies to drama.

Repetition of Verbal Strategy

It is not uncommon for a single character to use a particular verbal strategy (e.g., aggressive debate) throughout a whole play. The recurring strategy provides a rhythmic pulse both when the strategy is used boldly and the audience is aware of it and when it is used subtly and the audience is not aware that the same verbal maneuvering is being employed again and again. Playwrights often cross character lines and unite a play by assigning the same verbal strategy to several characters with variations. There are many methods of dealing with the universe, whether it is the large and unmanageable one of tragedy or the more limited and less demanding one of comedy. In *Semantics and Communication*, John C. Condon defines *symbolic strategies*, a term coined by Kenneth Burke. They are "the ways in which we may manipulate our symbols in lieu of altering reality. In one sense all of language and thought is a strategy for coming to symbolic terms with that muddled world of process and change. Every time we impose order on the outside world through language, we are applying some kind of strategy."[1] Verbal strategies may be as little important as the "how" of a character's attempt to accomplish some isolated task in a play or as vastly important as the "how" of many characters' attempts to deal with the world of the play.

An example of openly emphasized strategy which, although seated particularly in one character, applies to other characters of the play as well, may be found in the light comedy by Noel Coward, *Hay Fever*. Judith Bliss, the "retired" actress, has a habit of speech which we might call "talking herself into a role." She uses the scheme several times throughout the play with repeatedly humorous results. Her recurrent system of thought is comic, partly because it is recurrent (Bergson would say she becomes a kind of automaton), partly because our emotions are not engaged in any way, and partly because we have been made wholly aware of the pattern from the first. Her children point out to her (really to us) that she is always heading for a performance. And from that point on we come to expect it of her.

The following passage from act 1 is long because Judith is, after all, working herself into a role. She has just learned that her romantic weekend will be ruined because each other member of the family has invited a guest as well. In this case, the role she chooses is her most frequently recurring dramatic character, a combination of unappreciated mother, fading actress, and over-the-hill woman of the world. Simon and Sorel are used by Coward to point up Judith's strategy.

SOREL. . . . . I wish I were earning my own living somewhere—a free agent —able to do whatever I liked without being cluttered up and frustrated by the family—

JUDITH *(picturesquely)*. It grieves me to hear you say that, Sorel.

SOREL. Don't be infuriating, Mother!

JUDITH *(sadly)*. A change has come over my children of late. I have tried to shut my eyes to it, but in vain. At my time of life one must face bitter facts!

SIMON. This is going to be the blackest Saturday-till-Monday we've ever spent!

JUDITH *(tenderly)*. Sorel, you mustn't cry.

SOREL. Don't sympathize with me; it's only temper.

JUDITH *(pulling her down on to sofa beside her)*. Put your head on my shoulder, dear.

SIMON *(bitterly)*. Your head, like the golden fleece . . .

SOREL *(tearfully)*. Richard'll have to have "Little Hell" and that horrible flapper the Japanese room.

JUDITH. Over my dead body!

SIMON *(comes over to his mother)*. Mother, what are we to do?

JUDITH *(pulls him down on his knees and places his head on her right shoulder. SOREL's head on her left. Makes a charming little motherly picture)*. We must all be very, very kind to every one!

SIMON. Now then, Mother, none of that!

JUDITH *(aggrieved)*. I don't know what you mean, Simon.

SIMON. You were being beautiful and sad.

JUDITH. But I am beautiful and sad.

SIMON. You're not particularly beautiful, darling, and you never were.

JUDITH. Never mind; I made thousands think I was.

SIMON. And as for being sad—

JUDITH *(pushes SIMON on the floor)*. Now, Simon, I will not be dictated to like this! If I say I'm sad, I *am* sad. You don't understand, because you're precocious and tiresome. . . . There comes a time in all women's lives—

SOREL *(rises and stands at L. corner of sofa)*. Oh dear! *(With pained expression.)*

JUDITH. What did you say, Sorel?

SOREL. I said, "Oh dear!"

JUDITH. Well, please don't say it again, because it annoys me.

SOREL *(smiling)*. You're such a lovely hypocrite!

JUDITH *(casting up her eyes)*. I don't know what I've done to be cursed with such ungrateful children! It's very cruel at my time of life—

SIMON. There you go again!

JUDITH *(pause—inconsequently)*. You're getting far too tall, Sorel.[2]

Judith operates throughout the entire comedy with the same partial awareness that she is acting, but she cannot seem to help herself. When a situation becomes tense, she finds herself casting about for the appropriate lines, blocking, and fellow players which will make sense of the situation and build to a theatrical denouement. She needs to play scenes to afford her some measure of excitement and importance while she is "retired." Judith's most outrageous scenes occur in act 2. When her husband, David, insults her in front of guests and then proceeds to take the vamp, Myra, out to the garden, Judith finds herself alone with Richard Greatham, a diplomat, who was originally her daughter's weekend partner. The situation, slightly tense, requires a script. Judith makes her way through "brave, but beaten-down wife," "attractive mother who is being forced into shadow by an attractive daughter," "faded and weary romantic," and finally when this script has caught Richard and seduced him into an old-fashioned love scene, "romantic heroine who finds true love outside her marriage."

Judith uses her old familiar ploy, her recurring line, with Richard: "I've reached an age now when I just want to sit back and let things go on around me—and they do" (p. 38). Her constant references to her age have become familiar to us. Judith uses the ploy again later in act 2. She has just discovered Sandy, the young boxer who was originally her weekend partner, kissing her daughter in the library. In the "horrified mother" and "shunned romantic object" scenes, she resorts to, "It's far from easy, at my time of life, to . . . " The stage direction indicates that she begins to act at this point (p. 41). In this scene, as in others, Judith is only partially acting at first—making her way to a performance. When she finds her script for her confrontation with Sandy and Sorel, she plays it to the hilt, as they say. With sad magnanimity, she gives the young lovers to each other, much against their wills.

Coward's repetition of verbal strategy is a source of comedy in *Hay Fever*. But, as with all rhythmic patterns, it is also a source of meaning, light and frivolous though that meaning may be. We begin to notice that role-finding and role-playing are not peculiar to Judith. All the characters of *Hay Fever* indulge in the sport as well, with varying degrees of success. The obviousness of the strategy when Judith uses it is a factor in telling us to take it lightly. (Sartre and Pirandello made more bitter comedies of the same strategy.) In *Hay Fever* no one will be mortally wounded in the process of role-playing. At the most, certain of the characters will be made miserably uncomfortable, but not hurt.

Hay Fever is, needless to say, a frivolous comedy, meant for enjoyment and lacking in complex philosophical import. The rhythm of repeated verbal and behavioral strategy is utilized in almost every play, whether it is simple or complex of design. A more subtle repetition of verbal strategy is used by Chekhov in *Uncle Vanya*. Complex plays like *Hamlet, Uncle Vanya,* and *Waiting for Godot* provide examples of all kinds of rhythmic patterning. Since Chekhov's characters are so essentially selfish, their creator had to find methods of showing us their self-absorption rather than telling us about it. One of his schemes for doing so is the *inappropriate monologue*. Often a character launches into a long speech, the intent of which is self-explanation or self-justification. These speeches are practically public soliloquies and are inappropriate to the social context in which they appear. Anything may provoke these surprisingly lengthy explanations; often the provocation appears to be a careless comment or a simple question. However, the speaker of the monologue seems to take these apparently meaningless comments as insults or reproaches. In many cases the victim is correct. But the source and direction of the insults tends to be as much a mystery to the provoker as to the provoked. The speaker speaks his monologue because he finds the world blind and deaf to his particular sensibilities. In speaking the monologue, however, he becomes totally blind and deaf to the sensibilities of his audience. The speech is intended to satisfy the speaker in some way, to justify his emotions or his behavior to himself as well as to the blurred faces who make up his audience. There appear to be two methods of justifying self: by attacking others and by exposing to view carefully chosen "personal shortcomings" which only prove how much better than others the speaker really is. As repeated verbal strategy, the monologues are rhythmic in that their recurrence, the buildup to them, and the overall effects produced provide part of the patterning in motion of each Chekhovian play. There are two real soliloquies in *Uncle Vanya*. Both Vanya and Yelena speak to themselves, Vanya late at night in act 2, Yelena before her interview with Astrov in act 3. It is considered odd that soliloquies should disturb the atmosphere of a naturalistic play. But these soliloquies are not nearly so surprising or out of place in a

performance of the play as one might think. They flow rhythmically and naturally from something very like them which has
been repeated several times.

In act 1, for instance, Astrov asks Vanya, with what is mild
and good-natured teasing about his laziness, "Had a good
sleep?" After Vanya answers, "Yes . . . very," and yawns, Astrov is treated to an explanation of the altered household
schedule—the reasons for sleeping in midday. When Astrov
continues his "teasing" with "Tell us something. . . . Is there
nothing new? . . . And the Professor?" Vanya launches into an
incredibly long-winded attack on Serebryakov, the "old dry-as-
dust," who is "a learned fish" (pp. 195-96). Later in act 1 Astrov
is paying a good deal of attention to Yelena and is getting a good
deal of attention from the gathering in the garden. Sonya has
just repeated his theory of forestry almost word for word. So
Vanya attacks Astrov by belittling his work in forestry. His attack is made indirect by his joking and careless manner, but the
attack is not lost on Astrov. Moreover Yelena has been chal-
lenging him to offer some self-justification by finding his work
boring (p. 201). Astrov has been provoked, and what follows is a
long justification of himself, his work, his ideals.

Examples of the provoked monologue in *Uncle Vanya* are numerous. Yelena philosophizes when Vanya calls her indolent.
Astrov reviews his life when Sonya reproaches him for drinking. The lead-up of indirect attack and the result, *overjustifica-
tion*, are recurring verbal strategies. However, a second strategy, equally important and related to the one of self-justification
recurs in all the monologues. The monologue itself seems to follow a pattern. The speaker generally begins by recognizing
some previous comment, even answering the question which
preceded his speech, only to hit upon a phrase or a rhetorical
question which suddenly sets him in motion, as it were, impel-
ling him onward, until having found the appropriate rhetoric
for that idea and taxed the idea thoroughly with that rhetoric,
he generally runs out of steam. The characters of *Uncle Vanya*,
it seems, will talk themselves silly. They will ornament an idea

to extinction and tear a passion to tatters. Since they use word and phrase repetition (which we have already discussed), a few trimmed down examples should speak for themselves. Vanya's "twenty-five years" speech has already been cited (see above, p. 51). It is one of the play's best examples of runaway rhetoric that fizzles out.

The first example (or the establishment of the rhythm) occurs early in the play. Marina insinuates for the second time that Astrov is a bit too fond of vodka, as well as confirming the obvious: that he has aged in eleven years. Astrov patterns his rhetoric nicely until "It's inevitable." The subject of his moustache brings him back to earth for a moment, but it immediately becomes a new takeoff point for his rhetoric, a shorter spurt of it, anticlimactic and exhausted of its steam quickly.

ASTROV. Yes. . . . In ten years I have become a different man. And what's the reason of it? I am overworked, nurse. From morning till night I am always on my legs, not a moment of rest, and at night one lies under the bedclothes in continual terror of being dragged out to a patient. All these years that you have known me I have not had one free day. I may well look old! And the life in itself is tedious, stupid, dirty. . . . This life swallows one up completely. There are none but queer people about one—they are a queer lot, all of them—and when one has lived two or three years among them, by degrees one turns queer too, without noticing it. It's inevitable *(twisting his long moustache)*. Ough, what a hugh moustache I've grown . . . a stupid moustache. . . . I've turned into a queer fish, nurse. I haven't grown stupid yet, thank God! My brains are in their right place, but my feelings are somehow blunter. There is nothing I want, nothing I care about, no one I am fond of . . . except you, perhaps—I am fond of you *(kisses her on the head)*. I had a nurse like you when I was a child.

(Pp. 193–94)

In Astrov's act 1 "forestry" speech, he becomes minimally aware of Yelena and Vanya for a moment. But he has not yet spent his rhetoric in answering his own rhetorical question. He explains everything in series, as though he has learned his speech and said it many a time before. And he repeats himself about wild creatures and wasted resources. When the vodka arrives, he fizzles out and undercuts his tirade with self-irony. Through the speech he manages to put Vanya in the category of "unreflecting savage," therefore indicating his own worth by comparison. And he manages carefully—not consciously—to expose his own vulnerability to the meaning of a sapling:

VOYNITSKY *(laughing).* Bravo, bravo! That's all charming but not convincing; so *(to ASTROV)* allow me, my friend, to go on heating my stoves with logs and building my barns of wood.

ASTROV. You can heat your stoves with peat and build your barns of brick. Well, I am ready to let you cut down wood as you need it, but why destroy the forests? The Russian forests are going down under the axe. Millions of trees are perishing, the homes of wild animals and birds are being laid waste, the rivers are dwindling and drying up, wonderful scenery is disappearing never to return; and all because lazy man has not the sense to stoop down and pick up the fuel from the ground. *(To YELENA ANDREYEVNA)* Am I not right, madam? One must be an unreflecting savage to burn this beauty in one's stove, to destroy what we cannot create. Man is endowed with reason and creative force to increase what has been given him; but hitherto he has not created but destroyed. There are fewer and fewer forests, the rivers are drying up, the wild creatures are becoming extinct, the climate is ruined, and every day the earth is growing poorer and more hideous. *(To VOYNITSKY)* Here you are looking at me with irony, and all I say seems to you not serious and—perhaps I really am a crank. But when I walk by the peasants' woods which I have saved from cutting down, or when I hear the rustling of the young copse planted by my own hands, I realise that the climate is to some extent in my power, and that if in a thousand years man is to be happy I too shall have had some small hand in it. When I plant a birch tree and see it growing green and swaying in the wind my soul is filled with pride, and I . . . *(seeing the labourer, who has brought a glass of vodka on a tray).* However *(drinks),* it's time for me to go. Probably the truth of the matter is that I am a crank. I have the honour to take my leave! *(Goes towards the house.)* (Pp. 201–02)

Even Yelena resorts to rhetoric, to spinning out an idea. In addition to making evident her attraction to Astrov, the following speech operates to remind us of the double strategy the characters of this play use. Yelena tells Vanya, in effect, "you are destructive, I am sensitive." She, of course, does not say it simply.

VOYNITSKY. If you could see your face, your movements! You are too indolent to live! Ah, how indolent!

YELENA. Ach! indolent and bored! Everyone abuses my husband; everyone looks at me with compassion, thinking, "Poor thing! she has got an old husband." This sympathy for me, oh, how well I understand it! As Astrov said just now, you all recklessly destroy the forests, and soon there will be nothing left on the earth. In just the same way you recklessly destroy human beings, and soon, thanks to you, there will be no fidelity, no purity, no capacity for sacrifice left on earth! Why is it you can never look with indifference at a woman unless she is yours? Because—that doctor is right—there is a devil of destruction in all of you. You have no feeling for the woods, nor the birds, nor for women, nor for one another!

VOYNITSKY. I don't like this moralising.

(A pause.)

YELENA. That doctor has a weary, sensitive face. An interesting face. Sonya is evidently attracted by him; she is in love with him, and I understand her feeling. He has come three times since I have been here, but I am shy and have not once had a proper talk with him, or been nice to him. He thinks I am disagreeable. Most likely that's why we are such friends, Ivan Petrovitch, that we are both such tiresome, tedious people. Tiresome! Don't look at me like that, I don't like it.

(P. 203)

Chekhov's patterning of verbal strategy is subtly rhythmic and as a result subtly comic. Since Coward's pattern is more openly emphasized, it provokes a heartier sort of laughter. Part of Chekhov's pattern, the part in fact that spurs the audience to laughter, is the "loss of steam" or the intrusion of reality which finally undercuts each long exercise in self-expression and shows it up for what it is—a narcissistic verbal strategy for self-justification.

An even subtler use of repeated verbal strategy can be found (as what cannot) in *Hamlet*. It might be described as a *rhythm of inclusion*, and Shakespeare gives it a good deal of variety. An audience is likely to be aware of the pattern when Polonius uses it, and because they are aware, they will laugh. Hamlet, Claudius, and other serious characters use the strategy with varying degrees of subtlety and are likely to intrigue rather than amuse the audience.

The strategy of inclusion means fitting everything in. A character, to prove that what he is saying is just or true, stops in midthought to include additional items of proof, to insert subsidiary ideas, to explain contradictions. Bert States calls this strategy "compulsive 'documentation' " in "The Word-Pictures in *Hamlet*," an essay concerned with the abundance of information the play pours out on countless subjects and in numerous forms, moods, and shapes of grief. It is a habit in the play which "reaches into the very rhythm and logic of its development." Characters are not only "devoted to an elaboration of the elsewhere, the other, the previous, or the timeless," but also to delivering verbal " 'documents,' or essayistic set-speeches on natural law. . . . over and over, we find characters falling into a *seriatim* rhythm in which they seem compelled to inventory a thing or process within an inch of its life before passing on to more urgent matters."[3]

Insistent inclusion, as rhythm, ties the play together. Polonius, the most obvious user of the strategy, is the master of the parenthetical phrase. Although the text of his speech is punctuated in this edition without any parentheses, we could in fact, reset it with many. We could probably include sets within other sets. Polonius, like the Ghost, insists that he will be brief, only to contradict himself, just as everything he says can be contradicted. It is not enough for him to understand that this is the case. He immunizes against it:

POLONIUS.   This business is well ended.
  My liege, and madam, to expostulate
  What majesty should be, what duty is,

Why day is day, night night, and time is time,
Were nothing but to waste night, day, and time.
Therefore since brevity is the soul of wit,
And tediousness the limbs and outward flourishes,
I will be brief—your noble son is mad.
Mad call I it, for to define true madness,
What is't but to be nothing else but mad?
But let that go.

GERTRUDE.   More matter, with less art.

POLONIUS. Madam, I swear I use no art at all.
That he's mad 'tis true; 'tis true, 'tis pity,
And pity 'tis 'tis true—a foolish figure,
But farewell it, for I will use no art.
Mad let us grant him then, and now remains
That we find out the cause of this effect,
Or rather say, the cause of this defect,
For this effect defective comes by cause.
Thus it remains, and the remainder thus.
Perpend;
I have a daughter—have while she is mine—
Who in her duty and obedience, mark,
Hath given me this. Now gather and surmise.
  (Reads.)   (2.2.85–108)

Hamlet uses the pattern, or a cousin of it, to make sport of
Polonius by insisting on seeing everything there is to see in a
cloud. It is not surprising that he can get the foolish old counsel-
lor to agree with his observations. The agreement is motivated,
of course, by Polonius' playing along with the mad prince. But it
is appropriate that two of the detectives who play the same kind
of investigation game should play games with each other:

HAMLET. Do you see yonder cloud that's almost in shape of a camel?
POLONIUS. By th' mass and 'tis, like a camel indeed.
HAMLET. Methinks it is like a weasel.
POLONIUS. It is backed like a weasel.
HAMLET. Or like a whale?
POLONIUS. Very like a whale.   (3.2.392–98)

When Hamlet forces Horatio and Marcellus to swear never to reveal what they know of the Ghost, he includes in the oath every safeguard against a careless, fear-ridden, or intentional breaking of the oath. It is impressively legalistic. The strategy of inclusion in this scene is wholly serious as opposed to the previous two examples. The situation is serious, and the listeners do not quarrel with, but accept, the strategy. There is, in addition, a great deal of breakup to the rhythm of inclusion, for instance, the Ghost traveling beneath the stage, and the inclusion, too, of Hamlet's philosophical observations. Part of the rhythmic effect of the whole scene, indeed, is the inclusion of more and more detail by Hamlet as the oath proceeds, always punctuated by "swear":

HAMLET. Never make known what you have seen to-night.
HORATIO and MARCELLUS. My lord we will not.
HAMLET.   Nay but swear't.
HORATIO.   In faith
    My lord not I.
MARCELLUS.   Nor I my lord in faith.
HAMLET. Upon my sword.
MARCELLUS.   We have sworn my lord already.
HAMLET. Indeed, upon my sword, indeed.
GHOST. *(beneath).* Swear.
HAMLET. Ha, ha, boy, sayst thou so? Art thou there truepenny?
    Come on—you hear this fellow in the cellarage—
    Consent to swear.
HORATIO.   Propose the oath, my lord.
HAMLET. Never to speak of this that you have seen,
    Swear by my sword.
GHOST *(beneath).* Swear.
HAMLET. Hic et ubique? Then we'll shift our ground.
    Come hither gentlemen,
    And lay your hands again upon my sword.
    Swear by my sword,
    Never to speak of this that you have heard.
GHOST *(beneath).* Swear by his sword.

HAMLET. Well said old mole, canst work i' th' earth so fast?
   A worthy pioneer. Once more remove, good friends.
HORATIO. O day and night, but this is wondrous strange.
HAMLET. And therefore as a stranger give it welcome.
   There are more things in heaven and earth, Horatio,
   Than are dreamt of in your philosophy.
   But come—
   Here as before, never, so help you mercy,
   How strange or odd some'er I bear myself—
   As I perchance hereafter shall think meet
   To put an antic disposition on—
   That you at such times seeing me never shall,
   With arms encumbered thus, or this head-shake,
   Or by pronouncing of some doubtful phrase,
   As, well, well, we know—or, we could an if we would—
   Or, if we list to speak—or, there be an if they might,
   Or such ambiguous giving out, to note
   That you know aught of me—this do swear,
   So grace and mercy at your most need help you.
GHOST *(beneath)*. Swear.
   (They swear.)   (1.5.144–82)

Claudius uses the strategy of inclusion somewhat differently in his first speech of the play. His intent seems to be to immunize himself against disapprobation. His method is inclusion by paradox. By inclusion, he attempts to explain the "marriage" of discretion and nature. It is a cold speech, too consistently balanced to be believed. His marriage to Gertrude is paradoxical many times over: they married "with a defeated joy, / With an auspicious, and a dropping eye, / With mirth in funeral, and with dirge in marriage, / In equal scale weighing delight and dole" (1.2.10–13).

The rhythm of inclusion is part of the entire rhythm of *Hamlet*. There are many other examples, among them Polonius' instructions to Reynaldo, in which he covers all the possibilities of the reasons and the means for spying on Laertes; the clowns, who include all the possibilities (absurd though they may be) for accidental-suicidal drowning; Claudius, who lists the problems of his office—Polonius murdered, Hamlet gone, people gossiping, Ophelia mad, Laertes angry. It is "Like to a murdering-piece" (4.5.94). States points out many other varied and subtle examples of the process of inclusion at work in the play. Anything so much a process, a way of dealing with the universe, is bound to color the whole as rhythmically repetitive. The varied ways in which the process works provide the necessary changes. But the whole points to a progression, or in this case, perhaps, the *halting* of a progression. Kenneth Burke defines the strategy of *Hamlet* the play as one of ceaseless investigation. Hamlet is the sleuth who becomes more caught up with the method than with the result. He reasons before acting, or rather instead of acting. His mind becomes a court of law in which the evidence is weighed and weighed again. Even when Claudius is proved guilty of murder and corruption in the state of Denmark, the final sentence is delayed. More evidence is gathered, for the evidence itself is fascinating. As States points out, Hamlet is not alone in this world of insistent inclusion.[4] It is peopled by many others who look, and therefore find. The scheme of inclusion is an element in the overall strategy of delay.

Many a committee member has learned that insistent inclusion is an excellent way of becoming deeper in insight and slower in action. The rhythm of a repeated verbal strategy is perhaps one of the most important indicators in life of meaning, timing, ability to change, desire for change, and so forth. It is definitely one of the most important indicators of meaning in drama.

Patterning of Attitude

All rhythm inspires movement of some sort, but perhaps the simplest indicator of movement rhythm is attitude rhythm. I do not propose to discuss movement here, but simply to recognize that it must of necessity occur when a play is staged and should even occur in our imaginations as we read a play. To be sure, the "right" movement is one of the most exciting features of theatre. All the director's and actor's creativity in finding and executing the "right" movement is not to be minimized. The source of that creativity and the limits imposed upon it, however, come from the playwright's text. A director of college theatre is reported to have said that all plays consist of two kinds of lines which imply movement: "to" lines and "from" lines. This is no doubt a great simplification of both dramatic dialogue and stage movement, but as a starting point for understanding attitude rhythm it is useful.

I use *attitude rhythm* to mean some regular recurrence and alternation of positive and negative expressions. Positive attitudes include speaking *to* someone, *for* someone, *for* something, asking questions of, making verbal gestures toward, and so forth. These and their complements cover a great deal of territory. Negative attitudes include avoidance of another character, resistance to another character (grunts, groans, silence, brief remarks), verbal gestures directed away from another character, and simply the "secondary position" in a conversation.

The positive and negative attitudes are drama's battery

82

charges. They are complementary in producing energy. And they are complementary in producing conflict. Much of the time the playwright produces some consistent system of repetition and alternation in the charges. One or the other of the "charges" *appears* to be moving the scene, although both are of course necessary.

Early in *Waiting for Godot* we are clued into the fact that Vladimir is the more active, more hopeful character, and Estragon the more passive, more resigned. Vladimir wants conversation and communion, Estragon does not, or at least does not care one way or the other. Estragon's behavior is a perfect example of what John C. Condon calls "prevention of communication."[1]

VLADIMIR. . . . So there you are again.
ESTRAGON. Am I?
VLADIMIR. I'm glad to see you back. I thought you were gone forever.
ESTRAGON. Me too.
VLADIMIR. Together again at last! We'll have to celebrate this. But how?
   (He reflects.) Get up till I embrace you.
ESTRAGON *(irritably).* Not now, not now.   (P. 7)

The first build of the play continues in a related vein, until a temporary change is effected. It is at the end of the first build and the accent is the change: Vladimir stops pushing. He temporarily gives up and gives in. He says gloomily, "It's too much for one man." And after a pause, cheerfully, "On the other hand what's the good of losing heart now, that's what I say. We should have thought of it a million years ago, in the nineties" (p. 7). Vladimir is still the same character, still aggressively optimistic, but his attitude shift points out that he is momentarily thinking about himself and about life and, for the moment, leaving Estragon to himself.

The same attitudes repeat through much of the play. The stability of those attitudes and their occasional change is a rhythmic pattern. Estragon's negativity continually makes Vladimir try to *sell* optimism to Estragon and therefore to himself. Late in act 1, after the exit of the Boy, the following exchange occurs. It is a variation on the pattern.

VLADIMIR. We've nothing more to do here.

ESTRAGON. Nor anywhere else.

VLADIMIR. Ah Gogo, don't go on like that. Tomorrow everything will be better.

ESTRAGON. How do you make that out?

VLADIMIR. Did you not hear what the child said?

ESTRAGON. No.

VLADIMIR. He said that Godot was sure to come to-morrow. *(Pause.)* What do you say to that?   (P. 34)

The reunion of the tramps in act 2 repeats the pattern in an even stronger key, only to prepare us for an interesting reversal. Estragon's increased negativity is balanced by his giving up and giving in to his relief at having found Didi again:

VLADIMIR. You again! *(ESTRAGON halts but does not raise his head. VLADIMIR goes toward him.)* Come here till I embrace you.

ESTRAGON. Don't touch me!

   (VLADIMIR holds back, pained.)

VLADIMIR. Do you want me to go away? *(Pause.)* Gogo! *(Pause. VLADIMIR observes him attentively.)* Did they beat you? *(Pause.)* Gogo! *(ESTRAGON remains silent, head bowed.)* Where did you spend the night?

ESTRAGON. Don't touch me! Don't question me! Don't speak to me! Stay with me!   (P. 37)

This reversal in Estragon's attitude continues and is even further explained later: Estragon voices his emotional dependence, which is rare for him: "I heard you singing. . . . That finished me. I said to myself, He's all alone, he thinks I'm gone for ever, and he sings" (p. 38). The moving and comic effects of this passage are really the result of careful rhythmic preparation. We have come to expect no "soft" emotion or positive attitudes toward friendship from Estragon. But he is so violently negative at the start of act 2, that the natural balance, the natural progression is a reversal. Beckett has not altered Estragon's character of course. After his outburst, Estragon returns to his usual level of disapproval and resistiveness.

VLADIMIR. You must be happy too, deep down, if you only knew it.

ESTRAGON. Happy about what?

VLADIMIR. To be back with me again.

ESTRAGON. Would you say so?

VLADIMIR. Say you are, even if it's not true.

ESTRAGON. What am I to say?

VLADIMIR. Say, I am happy.

ESTRAGON. I am happy.

VLADIMIR. So am I.

ESTRAGON. So am I.

VLADIMIR. We are happy.

ESTRAGON. We are happy. *(Silence.)* What do we do now, now that we are happy?

VLADIMIR. Wait for Godot. (Pp. 38–39)

Rhythm through conflicting attitudes and attitude change is capable of all sorts of variation. It is related to patterns of sound and silence in many ways, but it is not the same thing, really. The negative charge is often expressed by silence or shorter lines than the positive charge. But when attitude change occurs, someone's mind has changed, even if temporarily, about some issue, or as in Estragon's case, about the risk involved in expressing a hidden attitude. When Horatio and Hamlet and Claudius break their silences it is because each of them has in some way "seen a ghost." Circumstances have changed to release the restraint. With attitude changes, though, we get the feeling that the important change is not specifically relative silence to sound, but aggression to submission or negativity to positivity or refusal to acceptance. Of course, they are related, more so even than other rhythmic patterns are.

In Ibsen's *The Master Builder* many of the most fascinating scenes are based on a positive-negative rhythm pattern. Solness is not only the master builder but the master of those people who surround him—his wife and his employees. The play opens with a discussion about him, in which the keynote is that he is someone to be feared, someone to be careful of. Yet in his scenes with Hilda, it is she who has the power, and it is she who controls the situation. She tells him what he said, felt, and did ten years ago. As she does so, in act 1, very soon after she has arrived, Solness listens, sometimes with amusement, always with interest. He plays a secondary part to her. He even makes every attempt to play along with her and to agree with her until she insists that he kissed her, ten years ago, when she was a girl of thirteen or thereabouts:

HILDA *(looks fixedly at him).* You came and kissed me, Mr. Solness.
SOLNESS *(open-mouthed, rising from his chair).* I did!
HILDA. Yes, indeed you did. You took me in both your arms, and bent my head back and kissed me—many times.
SOLNESS. Now really, my dear Miss Wangel—!
HILDA *(rises).* You surely cannot mean to deny it?
SOLNESS. Yes, I do. I deny it altogether!
HILDA *(looks scornfully at him).* Oh, indeed! (P. 243)

Solness is not up to the battle. He tries to reason with Hilda, to find other explanations, but she refuses even to move, let alone to answer him, until he gives in. He finally does, and the rhythm of her testing him out, and testing out her power in an interrogation scene, is an exciting one:

HILDA *(turns her head a little, but without looking at him).* Then you admit it now?
SOLNESS. Yes—whatever you like.
HILDA. You came and put your arms around me?
SOLNESS. Oh, yes!
HILDA. And bent my head back?
SOLNESS. Very far back.
HILDA. And kissed me?
SOLNESS. Yes, I did.
HILDA. Many times?
SOLNESS. As many as ever you like.
HILDA *(turns quickly towards him and has once more the sparkling expression of gladness in her eyes).* Well, you see, I got it out of you at last! (Pp. 243–44)

Solness' replies are open to interpretation. Different performances would include differing degrees of seriousness and

ironic playing into the game. But for all intents and purposes
Solness is in Hilda's power. Her power is evident through a
rhythmic change. She can control him through verbal seduc-
tiveness, silence, aggressive (if sprightly) interrogation. Her
power, or the extent of it, would not be nearly so clear were it
not for the change to silence. Through the silence, we are made
aware of the extent to which Solness will go to appease her. She
has been speaking for a particular interpretation of events; Solness has been resisting that interpretation. The pattern of this
scene reflects the entire pattern of the relationship between
Solness and Hilda. She was light and seductive in a childlike
way ten years ago. The situation did not seem important. A silence or separation of ten years intervened. Finally Hilda
makes her appearance again with new energy and a deadly ag-
gressiveness that appears harmless, but, of course, is not. It is
Solness' giving in to her wishes that eventually kills him. In this
case, the rhythmic pattern of an early scene between them reflects the rhythm of the entire action. The whole play moves
with the same progression. Hilda's lightness in act 1 is followed
by a relatively good capacity for listening in act 2. And yet she
is certainly gaining power in act 2, as Solness tells her his secret fears, his philosophy about why he will fall. By act 3 we see
a Hilda who is more passionate and intense than ever. She has
not given up her idea of seeing him up on the tower, and she of
course finally achieves her goal.

In act 3, a similar progression in miniature occurs again, re-
establishing the rhythm. The "charges" are made evident
through a series of questions and answers. Hilda has just discovered a well-kept secret: Aline grieves for jewels, lace, and
above all, nine beautiful dolls, but not particularly for the death
of her two sons. She can only be glad for them. In the following
scene, it seems Hilda cannot make up her mind what to do *with*
the secret or *about* it. Solness and Aline, like so many of Ibsen's
characters, have spent their lives living a lie. Hilda has a great
stock in Solness' being superhuman. Part of the progression is a
mirror of the scene from the first act. This time, however, when

Hilda breaks her silence, she does not light up the atmosphere with her intensity. It takes her a while to "love" Solness again, and when she does she expects even more from him as a result. Now he must climb the tower and he must claim her and he must build castles in the air. In other words, in terms of the play's irony, he must die. The following scene is interesting for its rhythmically patterned reversal, which because it does not lead to the kind of renewed intensity we have become accustomed to, signals us of an important change:

HILDA. What brings you up here just now?

SOLNESS. I caught sight of you from over there.

HILDA. But then you must have seen her too?

SOLNESS. I knew she would go at once if I came.

HILDA. Is it very painful for you that she should avoid you in this way?

SOLNESS. In one sense, it's a relief as well.

HILDA. Not to have her before your eyes?

SOLNESS. Yes.

HILDA. Not to be always seeing how heavily the loss of the little boys weighs upon her?

SOLNESS. Yes. Chiefly that.

(HILDA drifts across the verandah with her hands behind her back, stops at the railing and looks out over the garden.)

SOLNESS *(after a short pause).* Did you have a long talk with her?

(HILDA stands motionless and does not answer.)

SOLNESS. Had you a long talk, I asked?

(HILDA is silent as before.)

SOLNESS. What was she talking about, Hilda?

(HILDA continues silent.)

SOLNESS. Poor Aline! I suppose it was about the little boys.

HILDA *(a nervous shudder runs through her; then she nods hurriedly once or twice).*

SOLNESS. She will never get over it—never in this world. *(Approaches her.)* Now you are standing there again like a statue; just as you stood last night.

HILDA *(turns and looks at him, with great serious eyes).* I am going away.

(Pp. 273–74)

Ibsen's highly structured plays are based upon highly structured conflicts. He writes of the clash of will against will. His characters intellectualize and symbolize to such an extent that, as States says, they literally die for an idea. Ibsen does not often use word rhythm or poetic rhythm; speaker alternation is at times fairly regular, for even the long expositions of the past are done by questions and answers or exchanges of commentary. The conversations of Ibsen's characters fulfill the function of information giving and debate. In dialogue, then, his predominant rhythm is likely to be attitude rhythm. When a character changes his mind in an Ibsen play, it is not to be taken lightly.

A different kind of repetition of attitude rhythm can be isolated in Shakespeare's *Measure for Measure*. Isabella comes to Angelo to plead for her brother's life. It is a difficult situation for a nun, pleading for the life of a man sentenced to die for fornication. She begins her plea by separating her brother from his act, pleading without reference to Claudio's crime. Angelo, very much against pardoning Claudio, is a force to be overcome. Much of the progression of the scene is dependent upon a rhythm of verbal strategy. However, that will be readily apparent in discussing the scene with regard to its patterning of attitudes. Angelo's resistance to Isabella's pleas is evident from his lines in the early part of the scene. He is terse and negative in the extreme: "Maiden, no remedy; I will not do't; Look, what I will not, that I cannot do; He's sentenced, 'tis too late; Pray you be gone" (2.2.48–66). As Isabella pleads more emotionally— "Tomorrow? O, that's sudden. Spare him, spare him. / He's not prepared for death" (83–84)—Angelo begins to explain his position with more care: "The law hath not been dead, though it hath slept" (90). Only, however, when Isabella's argument changes from a plea *for* her brother to an attack *against* Angelo and his likes (a change from defense to offense), does Angelo begin to listen. The major change of the scene is Angelo's change of mind about Isabella. "She speaks, and 'tis such sense / That my sense breeds with't.—Fare you well." And a line later, "I will bethink me; come again to-morrow" (141–42, 144). We later find out what has moved him in his soliloquy. But it is the establishment of an attitude (on the part of each major character) and the interrelated changes of attitude which create the governing rhythm of the scene. The changes indicate the progression and the meaning of the scene. And as always, rhythm is based on a sense of balance. When Angelo's resistance gives way, it does so in such a way as to betray the controls he maintained in the first place. The rhythm of the scene would have been very different had Angelo explained his position and his philosophy of law in the early part of the scene. But Shakespeare had in mind (or in pen) a rhythm of very tensely dramatic reversals in this play.

Change of an established attitude is one of the most exciting dramatic rhythms. Shakespeare increases our pleasure by giving us a second Angelo and Isabella scene in which he uses much the same rhythm. And since, as Bayer asserts, there is mathematical perfection in rhythm, there is more of sameness about the second interview scene than at first meets the eye and ear. For instance, the scenes are almost exactly the same length. Both have "prologues" and "epilogues" of about 20 lines. And each scene runs 187 lines. It is Isabella in the second interview scene who is brief. When Angelo says her brother must die, she is ready to leave with "Even so. Heaven keep your honour" (2.4.34). But Angelo keeps luring her back with the witchery of words, the weapons of this play. He is suitor now and he speaks generally at first: "Might there not be a charity in sin / To save this brother's life?" (63–64). As he continues to speak for a proposition, his arguments become more and more personal. Finally he attacks her on the basis of her calling, as she did him:

ANGELO.   let me be bold;
   I do arrest your words. Be that you are,
   That is, a woman; if you be more, you're none.
   If you be one—as you are well expressed
   By all external warrants—show it now,
   By putting on the destined livery.   (133–38)

As Isabella comes to understand Angelo's meaning, she lashes out, threatening him: "I will proclaim thee, Angelo; look for't" (151). But Angelo delivers his own ultimatum and threat. If she does not "yield up" her body, not only will he kill her brother, but he will torture him as well. And so, the second interview scene, a repetition of the first in several basic ways, is also a very ironic variation on the first. The rhythmic pattern is the same but its players' roles are reversed. And the conclusion of the second scene is of course vastly different from the first. It points the arrows of our expectation in a different direction: When and how will Angelo be found out? What will happen to Claudio? It is ironic that Angelo and Isabella progress to one point which mirrors the first scene. Again she must come tomorrow, this time to give an answer rather than to get one.

Isabella's soliloquy rounds out the pattern, for Angelo spoke the soliloquy at the end of the first scene. As in other examples of rhythmic patterning, the second scene has a rhythm of its own based upon recurrences and change. But the two scenes mirror each other in construction (rhythm at a standstill). Both scenes work toward a larger rhythmic effect of the whole play. That change of attitude should be a keynote is appropriate, for *Measure for Measure* is a dark comedy in which people influence each other as much with something beyond words as with words themselves. Neither the persuasive stance nor the reversal of suppliant/judge positions is peculiar to these scenes alone: the Duke as Friar is no longer an official power and is very much at the mercy of others; Isabella is Claudio's judge when he begs for his life. Recurrence and change of attitude is a factor in all plays. In dramas of clashing wills, however, it seems to be an extremely important rhythm. For instance, attitude change is a more important measure of the action in *Oedipus Rex* than in *Hamlet*. That is an extremely broad generalization, granted. But we measure *Oedipus* very much by its protagonist's mounting and decreasing hope and his rising and subsiding rages. We measure *Hamlet* more by the emergence of what is consistent (speaker alternation patterns, verbal strategies) because the play is so full of changes, so laden with changes, that it forces us to pick out and examine what is similar. These similar elements, juxtaposed, provide the play's irony. On the other hand, attitude rhythm provokes certain dramatic questions: Who will change? What will it take to change him? How long will it take? Will the change be permanent? Once we recognize an established attitude by its recurrence, we immediately expect some change as a balance.

Style

Every sort of rhythm discussed so far has depended to a great extent on style or "the voice of the author himself," as Northrop Frye defines it.[1] Patterns of word repetition, speaker alternation, attitude change, and verbal strategy generally indicate *how* a thing is said, *how* an act is accomplished. But overall consistency of style in a play (with of course appropriate variations) is a manifestation of an overall rhythmic pattern which gives a pulse to the whole work. Frye explains that "every writer has his own rhythm, as distinctive as his handwriting, and his own imagery, ranging from a preference for certain vowels and consonants to a preoccupation with two or three archetypes."[2] So long as the audience or reader is affected by style as a constant, style is operating rhythmically, that is, the author is speaking to us rhythmically.

The Greek tragic poets speak to us rhythmically precisely because their poetry is not only metrical but is stylistically consistent in singing out an idea. Scholars tell us that Aeschylus was consistently lyrical; Sophocles was less lyrical, but beautiful in a more logical sense; Euripides was less grand in style than the other two, writing a more emotionally and psychologically based poetry.

The Elizabethan dramatist's alternation between verse and prose is itself rhythmic. "In Elizabethan drama the center of gravity, so to speak, is somewhere between verse *epos* and prose, so that it can move easily from one to the other depending on the requirements of decorum, which are chiefly the social rank of the character and the genre of the play."[3] Moreover, the alternation between prose and verse moves us emotionally and indicates meanings. In Shakespeare's Measure for Measure, after the Duke's beautifully poetic and calming "Be absolute for death" speech (3.1.5–41), Isabella arrives at the prison. Her entrance is marked with an interruption of the verse with prose which begins to move the scene in a different rhythm, lending it a more nervous and jagged quality. When she begins to talk to Claudio, Shakespeare returns us to blank verse, which slows the scene down somewhat and renders it more formal. Yet the blank verse is very much broken up, partly by alternation of speaker in midline, or midrhythm, which causes it to retain some of the jagged quality of the prose introduction. These rhythmically stylistic changes are appropriate, for in the portion of the scene in which Shakespeare breaks up the verse, Isabella must tell her brother that she will not "die"—give up her chastity—to save his life. Only part of the scene follows, enough to illustrate the careful establishment of verse, the odd sense of formality it achieves in this particular scene, and the sense of tension, of emotions unexpressed as the metrical line is divided between Claudio and Isabella:

ISABELLA. What ho! Peace here; grace and good company.
PROVOST. Who's there? Come in, the wish deserves a welcome.
DUKE. Dear sir, ere long I'll visit you again.
CLAUDIO. Most holy sir I thank you.
ISABELLA. My business is a word or two with Claudio.
PROVOST. And very welcome. Look signior, here's your sister.
DUKE. Provost, a word with you.
PROVOST. As many as you please.
DUKE. Bring me to hear them speak, where I may be concealed.
(Exeunt DUKE and PROVOST)
CLAUDIO. Now sister, what's the comfort?
ISABELLA. Why,
    As all comforts are; most good, most good indeed.

Lord Angelo, having affairs to heaven,
Intends you for his swift ambassador,
Where you shall be an everlasting leiger.
Therefore your best appointment make with speed;
To-morrow you set on.

CLAUDIO.   Is there no remedy?

ISABELLA. None, but such remedy as, to save a head,
To cleave a heart in twain.

CLAUDIO.   But is there any?

ISABELLA. Yes, brother, you may live.
There is a devilish mercy in the judge,
If you'll implore it, that will free your life,
But fetter you till death.

CLAUDIO.   Perpetual durance?

ISABELLA. Ay, just—perpetual durance, a restraint,
Though all the world's vastidity you had,
To a determined scope.   (3.1.44–70)

Shakespeare, no one disputes, uses the verse-prose combination with extraordinary versatility. Yet he was following a form for drama in Elizabethan England just as the tragic poets of Greece were following established patterns. In each case, there was an accepted general style of the day. Yet each playwright of both periods automatically gave the literary style his own personal style.

Even the realistic and naturalistic styles are just that—styles. As such, they are capable of a great deal of variety. We may at times lump Ibsen and Strindberg together under a heading "realism" which indicates for convenience some similarities in production style, for instance, a sense of the time scheme and space scheme of daily life through purified and very carefully selected detail. And, for instance, a sense of linear action, or what Kenneth Burke calls "syllogistic progression" in the playing out of the plot. "To go from A to E through stages B, C and D is to obtain such form."[4] Though translations may vary, Ibsen's voice tends to be more polite, Strindberg's more savage. There is deadly irony beneath both Ibsen's restraint and Strindberg's slightly more emotional prose. Ibsen's protagonists are less likely to break down, weep, or do dances of grotesque death before our eyes. Ibsen's characters die theatrically but with a great deal of artfulness. They retire to other rooms (Hedvig and Hedda) or they climb distant towers (Solness) or take their time by fading out (Oswald). Strindberg's Captains of both *The Father* and *The Dance of Death* expose us to their quite violent death throes. The dialogue supports these differences in dramatic action. Here is an example from Ibsen's *Hedda Gabler* of a very carefully phrased and restrained cat-and-mouse game. The exchange is representative of Ibsen. In the final scene of the play Brack is blackmailing Hedda with his knowledge that the pistol that killed Lövborg belonged to her:

HEDDA. But I have nothing to do with all this repulsive business.

BRACK. No. But you will have to answer the question: Why did you give Eilert Lövborg the pistol? And what conclusions will people draw from the fact that you did give it to him?

HEDDA *(lets her head sink)*. That is true. I did not think of that.

BRACK. Well, fortunately, there is no danger, so long as I say nothing.

HEDDA *(looks up at him)*. So I am in your power, Judge Brack. You have me at your beck and call, from this time forward.

BRACK *(whispers softly)*. Dearest Hedda—believe me—I shall not abuse my advantage.

HEDDA. I am in your power none the less. Subject to your will and your demands. A slave, a slave then! *(Rises impetuously)* No, I cannot endure the thought of that! Never!

BRACK *(looks half-mockingly at her)*. People generally get used to the inevitable. (Pp. 219–20)

In Strindberg's *The Father* is an example of a more emotionally open game of cat-and-mouse. The Pastor is accusing Laura of "murder" in act 3:

PASTOR. You are strong, Laura, incredibly strong. You are like a fox in a trap, you would rather gnaw off your own leg than let yourself be caught! Like a master thief—no accomplice, not even your own conscience. Look at yourself in the glass! You dare not!

LAURA. I never use a looking glass!

PASTOR. No, you dare not! Let me look at your hand. Not a tell-tale blood stain, not a trace of insidious poison! A little innocent murder that the law cannot reach, an unconscious crime—unconscious! What a splendid idea! Do you hear how he is working up there? Take care! If that man gets loose he will make short work of you.

LAURA. You talk so much you must have a bad conscience. Accuse me if you can!

PASTOR. I cannot.

LAURA. You see! You cannot, and therefore I am innocent.[5]

Ibsen's rhythm provides for an ordering or controlling of emotion. Strindberg's allows for more expression of tension.

Chekhov and Gorki might even under some circumstances be related to each other as "naturalistic" stylists when the object of the lumping together is some explanation of associative action, or "naturalistic flow," or the juxtapositional approach. In terms of the time scheme and space scheme of daily life, they might be said to operate with an abundance of "seemingly" unselected detail. Their progressions too might both be described in Burke's term, "qualitative." One incident does not lead to another, so much as "the presence of one quality prepares us for the introduction of another. . . . Such progressions are qualitative rather than syllogistic as they lack the pronounced anticipatory nature of the syllogistic progression. We are prepared less to demand a certain qualitative progression than to recognize its rightness after the event. We are put into a state of mind which another state of mind can appropriately follow."[6]

In *The Lower Depths* Gorki speaks with the appearance of objectivity, but his voice invites us to pity, while Chekhov, in *The Cherry Orchard,* for instance, speaks to us with constant and sustained irony and invites us to laugh as we wince. When the Actor of *The Lower Depths*—drunk, desperate, and alone—has a brief and accidental meeting with Natasha in act 2, he rambles. The situation is sordid. Anna has just died of consumption; her corpse is only a few feet away from them, but they do not yet know she is dead. The Actor's reference to Ophelia is brief and is resolved by a reference to *King Lear.*

THE ACTOR. . . . Natasha, farewell—right—farewell!

NATASHA *(entering).* Don't wish me farewell, before you've wished me how-d'you-do!

THE ACTOR *(barring her way).* I am going. Spring will come—and I'll be here no longer—

NATASHA. Wait a moment! Where do you propose going?

THE ACTOR. In search of a town—to be cured—And you, Ophelia, must go away! Take the veil! Just imagine—there's a hospital to cure—ah —organisms for drunkards—a wonderful hospital—built of marble —with marble floors . . . light—clean—food—and all gratis! And a marble floor—yes! I'll find it—I'll get cured—and then I shall start life anew. . . . I'm on my way to regeneration, as King Lear said. Natasha, my stage name is . . . Svertchkoff—Zavoloushski . . . do you realize how painful it is to lose one's name? Even dogs have their names.[7]

Chekhov has Lopahin refer to Ophelia in *The Cherry Orchard.* His reference, however, is a painfully comic one because it is a very patterned one. The scene occurs in act 2. A wayfarer has just frightened Lyubov's family and friends. She has handled the scene, as she does all scenes, by giving her money away, in this case a gold piece to the wayfarer. Chekhov patterns this brief exchange to point to several ironies at once: Lyubov's inability to face reality, especially concerning money and the orchard; Lyubov's insensitivity to Varya; Lopahin's unintentional destructiveness both to Varya and to Lyubov's whole family with the cherry orchard as the central symbol. The exchange resolves itself associatively and ironically. "Ophelia" has dreamt of the religious life. Lopahin's sins to her (Varya) are twofold: his inability to marry her and his ability to buy the orchard. And best of all, Lopahin is simply cheering everyone up, reducing his own and everyone else's tension. He does not know what he is saying. He saw a "funny" play, the lines of which keep recurring to him.

LYUBOV. There's no doing anything with me. I'm so silly! When we get home, I'll give you all I possess. Yermolay Alexeyevitch, you will lend me some more . . . !

LOPAHIN. I will.

LYUBOV. Come, friends, it's time to be going. And Varya, we have made a match of it for you. I congratulate you.

VARYA *(through her tears)*. Mamma, that's not a joking matter.

LOPAHIN. "Ophelia, get thee to a nunnery!"

GAEV. My hands are trembling; it's a long while since I had a game of billiards.

LOPAHIN. "Ophelia! Nymph, in thy orisons be all my sins remember'd."

LYUBOV. Come, it will soon be supper-time.

VARYA. How he frightened me! My heart's simply throbbing.

LOPAHIN. Let me remind you, ladies and gentlemen: on the 22nd of August the cherry orchard will be sold. Think about that! Think about it! (P. 91)

Style is particularly evident in certain kinds of comedy. Frye discusses the fact that comedies of wit and manners often employ an epigrammatic style "in which something of the antithetical and repetitive structure of rhetorical prose" is evident.[8] Oscar Wilde's *The Importance of Being Earnest* is a good example of the epigrammatic style based upon antithesis and repetition. The author's voice is more than clear. Indeed we could hardly confuse his deliciously perverse humor in *The Importance of Being Earnest* with that of any other writer or any other play. Wilde's style, repeated and recurrent, is very much based on an inflection pattern which provides a rhythm that turns the world upside down and, we might almost say, makes the play repeatedly stand on its head.

Wilde perpetuates the rhythm of reversal in many ways throughout the play, and he juggles all the ways with such quickness and dexterity that the pace is that of a patter song. Some of the important variations on his voice or style are (1) reversal of expectation, (2) spoken reversal of common philosophy, (3) reversal of intention or peripety (characters are hoist by their own petards), and (4) reversal of direction in thought through antithesis or understatement or overstatement. Of course, all four methods listed are not only related, but are in their actual use juggled and overlapped constantly.

Reversal of expectation is used a good deal. At the very beginning of the play, when Algernon accuses Lane of stealing champagne, we expect the master to be somewhat concerned or irritated, the servant to be somewhat guilty and evasive. We get the opposite:

ALGERNON. . . . Oh! . . . by the way, Lane, I see from your book that on Thursday night, when Lord Shoreman and Mr. Worthing were dining with me, eight bottles of champagne are entered as having been consumed.

LANE. Yes, sir; eight bottles and a pint.

ALGERNON. Why is it that at a bachelor's establishment the servants invariably drink the champagne? I ask merely for information.

LANE. I attribute it to the superior quality of the wine, sir. I have often observed that in married households the champagne is rarely of a first-rate brand.[9]

Casualness and candor replace anger and guilt. The language is formally structured and there is reversal even in the phrasing. Algernon does not say, "We are supposed to have drunk eight bottles of champagne," which would have been less comic and less "casual" than what he does say. His reversal of the logical order of subject and object gives the bottles of champagne a crazy life of their own.

When Algernon philosophizes about the lower classes a few lines later, he reverses common philosophy. "Lane's views on marriage seem somewhat lax. Really, if the lower orders don't set us a good example, what on earth is the use of them? They seem, as a class, to have absolutely no sense of moral responsibility" (p.291). There is no doubt at this early point in the play that the world will continually be turned upside down.

A few moments later, a new variation of the reversal principle makes itself obvious. Jack, in trying to evade Algernon's questions, gets caught in his own trap. In this reversal of intention, Jack's airy evasions show him up as either a liar or a fool:

ALGERNON. . . . Where have you been since last Thursday?

JACK. . . . In the country.

ALGERNON. What on earth do you do there?

JACK. . . . When one is in town one amuses oneself. When one is in the country one amuses other people. It is excessively boring.

ALGERNON. And who are the people you amuse?

JACK (airily). Oh, neighbours, neighbours.

ALGERNON. Got nice neighbours in your part of Shropshire?

JACK. Perfectly horrid! Never speak to one of them.

ALGERNON. How immensely you must amuse them!   (P. 291)

This short exchange utilizes not only the reversal of intention, but the reversal of antithetical phrasing—Jack's parallel construction in the lines about the town and country are used to point opposites. Algernon uses the method again only a moment later. When he upbraids Jack for his flirtatious behavior, he immediately upends the attack with a reversal in the form of an antithetical understatement: "My dear fellow, the way you flirt with Gwendolen is perfectly disgraceful. It is almost as bad as the way Gwendolen flirts with you" (p. 291). This indeed is a style of repetitive and rhetorically phrased prose. The pattern of witty reversal is so constant throughout the play that it creates an overall rhythm of bright, aphoristic, intelligent nonsense, which proves itself by its constant repetition as sensible and true as anything else. The language also creates an expectation for reversals of all kinds. Since anything can reverse itself, it is no surprise that all single people end up altar-bound, lost identities are found, friends become brothers and enemies friends, and lies become truths.

Other writers of comedy utilize some of the same principles of reversal that Wilde does, although rarely in such obvious and overwhelming abundance. Yet, as Frye reminds us, the epigrammatic prose style that substitutes for verse in expressing "dignity, passion, witty imagery . . . and pathos," depends upon rhetorical tradition. "Nearly all the great writers of English comedy from Congreve to O'Casey have been Irishmen, and the rhetorical tradition survived longer in Ireland. The dramatic prose of Synge also ranks as literary mannerism, even if it does reproduce the speech rhythms of Irish peasantry."[10] The use of reversal and antithesis for comic (and tragic) effect is certainly evident in Sean O'Casey's *The Plough and the Stars*. His style is quite different from Wilde's, and the materials of which he makes his plays are different as well. Therefore his overall rhythm is far different from Wilde's or from anyone else's for that matter. But a part of O'Casey's pattern, a part of his major rhythm, is made up as Frye indicates of a rhythm of repetitive, rhetorical, antithetical phrasing.

Mrs. Gogan's early description of Nora Clitheroe in act 1 is an excellent example of antithetical phrasing used for comic effect:

FLUTHER. She's a pretty little Judy, all the same.

MRS. GOGAN. Ah, she is, an' she isn't. There's prettiness an' prettiness in it. I'm always sayin' that her skirts are a little too short for a married woman. An' to see her, sometimes of an evenin', in her glad-neck gown would make a body's blood run cold. I do be ashamed of me life before her husband. An' th' way she thries to be polite, with her "Good mornin', Mrs. Gogan," when she's goin' down, an' her "Good evenin', Mrs. Gogan," when she's comin' up. But there's politeness an' politeness in it.

FLUTHER. They seem to get on well together, all th' same.

MRS. GOGAN. Ah, they do, an' they don't. . . .[11]

Fluther has two particular verbal quirks which keep recurring: the words *derogatory* (which he generally misuses) and *vice versa*. *Vice versa* makes an excellent verbal cousin to Jinnie Gogan's *'tis* and *'tisn'ts*. Of Peter, Fluther says in act 1, "Take no notice of him. . . . You'd think he was dumb, but when you get his goat, or he has a few jars up, he's vice versa" (p. 637). And when he tries to calm Mrs. Gogan down just as she is about to enter into a fistfight in the barroom, in act 2, he says, "Now Jinnie, Jinnie, it's a derogatory thing to be smirchin' a night like this with a row; it's rompin' with th' feelin's of hope we ought to be, instead o' being vice versa!" (p.648). O'Casey's brilliance is his ability to take a comic device and reverse its effect, so that it becomes part of the tragic dimension of this play.

Mollser's coffin is about to be carried out for burial in act 4. It is a delicate moment. Bessie Burgess is too exhausted to stand to pay her final respects. Fluther's phrase becomes the source of tragic understatement:

BESSIE *(from the chair).* It's excusin' me you'll be, Mrs. Gogan, for not stannin' up, seein' I'm shaky on me feet for want of a little sleep, an' not desirin' to show any disrespect to poor little Mollser.

FLUTHER.   Sure, we all know, Bessie, that it's vice versa with you. (P. 661)

Although the comic characters use rhetorical speech, including reversals, quite obviously, O'Casey assigns the pattern in a more subtle form to the "serious" characters. Nora and Jack speak poetically and rhetorically *about* life's reversals:

NORA *(coquettishly removing his arm from around her).* Oh, yes, your lit-tle, little red-lipped Nora's a sweet little girl when th' fit seizes you; but your little, little red-lipped Nora has to clean your boots every mornin', all the same.

CLITHEROE *(with a movement of irritation).* Oh, well, if we're goin' to be snotty!
  (A pause.)

NORA.   It's lookin' like as if it was you that was goin' to be . . . snotty! Bridlin' up with bittherness, th' minute a body attempts t'open her mouth.

CLITHEROE.   Is it any wondher, turnin' a tendher sayin' into a meanin' o' malice an' spite!   (P. 642)

The rhythm of O'Casey's style permeates every moment of the play. The poetry of the Dublin tenements points to the tragic dimensions of the play (the ironic reversals of the rebellion) as well as to the comic dimensions (the eternal perversity of mankind).

If literary style is the man,[12] when we discuss style we are really making every attempt to describe the personal rhythm of the artist as he wrote a particular work, for somewhere in us we understand that his personal rhythm permeates every moment of his product. We force ourselves (as contemporary critics) to look only at the rhythm and to avoid biographical clues as to the man. Biographical criticism is deemed inadequate and "outdated," although it may (and probably will) come into fashion again if only out of nostalgia or boredom with the prevailing fashion. It seems to me, however, that biographical criticism as such really is inadequate, for men change daily, and every man's personal rhythm has many disguises. Yet criticism often boils down to trying to find some part of the author behind the works. When we study the artist's words, his meanings, his juxtapositions, we are really, as Frye says, dealing with the voice of the man, which though submerged to a great extent in drama, cannot be submerged totally. We are either rejecting or condescending toward or accepting of the *man* in various moods and frames of mind. Shakespeare is perhaps the most universally loved man of literature that ever existed. Flaubert called him "a continent,"[13] and others have searched for spectacular adjectives and nouns to describe his comprehensive intelligence and understanding, at least while writing. People are either bored by or irritated with Chekhov, or they fall passionately in love with him. Some see the position of his mouth as a gently ironic smile, while others see it as a condescending smirk, and a few even as a malevolent leer. To some his jokes are obscure and boring; to others they have the mark of genius. Some scholars, critics, and teachers are content to visit him once a year in the course of business. Others return to him often, for pleasure, and some are even drawn—like his family, his sister Masha in particular—to devote much of their lives to him. Wilde's letters tell us that there is something of *his* personal rhythm in *The Importance of Being Earnest*. This story from Chekhov's life tells us that some part of Chekhov's personal rhythm or pattern of speaking and reacting was repeated in his plays as a method of patterning dramatic action and pointing up meanings. Here is one biographer's account of the man:

Always receptive to genuine people, Chekhov for all his gentleness was capable of being ironic and occasionally even savage with those who were filled with their own importance. He loathed pretense, smug stupidity, militant vulgarity. One day, according to Gorky, three elegant ladies—magnificently dressed and over-perfumed—went to visit him and persisted in besetting him, and demanding the same in return, with "interesting observations" on the current Greek-Turkish war: all that he talked about was jellies. This was his way of getting rid of self-infatuated intruders. A pompous prosecutor who was trying to lure him into a discussion on judicial administration was politely asked whether he liked gramophones. The worst victims were those ladies of fashion who were determined at all costs—this had become something of a convention—to hold "Chekhovian" conversations with him. When one of them, with labored sighs, told him how gray and monotonous life was and what anxiety troubled her soul, adding "It's a sickness," he retorted: "Of course it's a sickness! In Latin it's called *morbus affectationis*."[14]

All the foregoing was intended as an investigation of certain sources of rhythm in dialogue. Categories sometimes overlap and examples often illustrate several kinds of rhythm in addition to the type under examination at the moment. Every playwright uses more than one source of dialogue rhythm. And dialogue rhythm is only part of the rhythm of an entire work. However, I have tried to illustrate throughout the *nonaccidental* quality of rhythms of every sort. No matter how small a part of the total pattern, each manifestation of rhythm is an intrinsic part of the whole, directing us, in Boleslavsky's words "to the final aim of the artist." In each case, the word, phrase, attitude, pattern of alternation, verbal strategy, or manifestation of style is repeated twice at least, and usually far more often than twice. Repetition provides a constant which makes us aware of and able to perceive change. And often, the changes are so patterned (repeated, reproduced) as to create a constant in themselves. Repetitions and changes arrange themselves into progressions and it is through progressions that we apprehend meaning and experience dramatic action.

The Single Scene

Throughout most of the history of theatre, before our own era, playwrights wrote for a stage which was in a sense already designed for them. The world views of their respective societies, as well as theatrical tradition, bequeathed to the playwrights accepted scenic conventions for the staging of their works. Limitations of a practical nature, as well as of custom, have always faced the playwright. However, in any good play, the idea of the scene, and the use of the scene, whatever the style may have been, is a rhythmic use and is therefore a part of the meaning of the entire dramatic work.

I am using the word *scene* to mean the setting or place when the playwright has chosen a *single* visual metaphor for his drama. The place might be abstract or real, spare or detailed, according to the needs of the action. It might be Vienna, Rome, the battlements, the palace at Thebes, an attic, or a country road.

Can a single scene or background to action be rhythmic? Can anything, in fact, that is stable and to the naked eye static, be rhythmic? Boleslavsky's Creature asked him about rhythm in stationary objects. In answering her, Boleslavsky arrives at the conclusion that there is not a stone in the universe without a sense of rhythm:

THE CREATURE. . . . One more question. On the canvas of the "Last Supper" the hands change, but at the same time they are stationary. How

106

can you apply the word Rhythm to them? Isn't Rhythm applied to movement?

BOLESLAVSKY. There is no limitation. A glacier moves two inches in a century; a swallow flies two miles in a minute—they both have Rhythm. Expand the idea from the glacier to a theoretical standstill and from the swallow to a theoretical light-speed. Rhythm will include and carry them all within its scope. To exist is to have Rhythm.[1]

Boleslavsky's examples tell us more than his philosophies do. The hands in the *Last Supper* and the variations in the color blue in Gainsborough's *Blue Boy* are examples of stable elements that change and therefore provide progression. But a glacier or a stone does not explain itself to us as easily. If a stone has rhythm, we should be able to describe it in some way. For one thing, the very stability of a stone provokes certain questions from an observer with a philosophical bent: How long since it has moved? How long until it will move again? What is moving within it? What forces from above, below, beyond, beside, and within it will make it move? In what ways can it change? Can it increase in mass, decrease in mass, split, shatter, crumble to dust? What forces will cause the stone to react in each of these ways? What is the relationship between what does happen to it and what possibly could happen to it?

A single scene (or single set) in a play can be rhythmic by constantly reminding us of its potential, by filling us with expectation of some change to come, by focusing our attention on smaller changes by which the scene "changes," and by showing us events happening upon it.

Even if we were to look at a stage or a "scene" for the moment without its characters or its action (as we do fairly often in the contemporary theatre when the scene is exposed before the start of the action), we would see something that is rhythmic in the sense that a painting is rhythmic. Certain regular features recur—colors, shapes, sizes, masses, direction of lines, and so on. Other features provide variety and contrast, and as a result some progression is indicated. We do not really look at the whole thing at once, or take in the whole thing at once, and as we look, our eyes move in rhythmic sweeps over the masses and spaces. The stage presents itself in logical groupings just as sentences present themselves (or words in sentences) in logical groupings.

Adolph Appia's designs, which he calls "Rhythmic Spaces,"[2] are excellent examples of repetition, change, and progression in the visual arts. We have the artist's word for it that it is meant to be rhythmic. Columns, levels, spaces repeat in design. The spaces invite action. Our eyes follow the lines formed by shadows, masses repeated, the linear form of steps. There is alternation between mass and space, and we are forced to be aware of what is solid and what is free. It would be hard to expect "petty actions" in any of these spaces, and difficult to expect unemotional actions. We are forced constantly to look at horizontal lines upon which something can happen and at the "spaces" framed by vertical lines which will encompass that action.

Any stage space tells us what is stable and what is free, how action will be framed, in what patterns the human body can move. The first example of a single scene that comes to mind, of course, is the stage for ancient Greek tragedy. No matter how many arguments we find that the law of "single place" in Greek tragedy is a myth, the fact remains that it is the "rule," the most commonly used visual representation in the extant tragedies. And what changes might have existed were apparently minimal —the shifting, perhaps, of periaktoi. So the Greek stage operated primarily with a single visual representation. From what we surmise about the stage for Greek tragedy, what rhythmic spaces does it provide? What is solid and what is free? What is stable and what may change? The skene, or permanent scenic background, is solid. But a repeated element in it is the entryway. There were apparently three of them in the skene, two on either side (in the skene or paraskenia) of a main central doorway. The central doorway, not only because of its centrality but because of its focus in a balance, received a certain amount of attention. Doorways provide potential space. The skene was symmetrical, its doorways were symmetrical, and so were the other entrances, the parodoi. These symmetrical passages, like arrows, pointed attention on the orchestra, a circle for performance, an open space which was unprotected, but backed by an image of solidity and grandeur.

Moreover, the "image" of the entire place could be changed or affected by forces from above, below, or within. Not only was the sky visible throughout a whole performance, but a machine (mechane) could bring gods into the action. The ground, a focal point of attention, could yield up ghosts or spirits by way of a tunnel known as Charon's steps. The ghost of Clytemnestra probably made its appearance from this underground entrance in the Eumenides. Horrors from within the temple or palace could be revealed by way of the ekkyklema, the wagon that emerged from the central doorway, generally complete with corpse.

A clearer understanding of the rhythm of this stage in use can be afforded by a look at the most famous of ancient tragedies, Oedipus Rex. Sophocles did not choose his set, except by naming it the palace at Thebes. He used what was available to him, though, in a rhythmic and ironic way. The stationary image of a place—the facade of a grand palace—is symbolic of the societal standing and public image of the protagonist. It reminds us that Oedipus was banished from this place once, that he inhabits the place at the present, and that he will be banished from the place once more. Neither the mechane nor Charon's steps is used in Oedipus. Only the human entryways are used—the doorways and parodoi. Oedipus, as investigator of his own identity as well as of the murderer of Laius, must piece together his history with information brought to the circle of focus from various witnesses. The first comes from without: Creon arrives from Delphi. Succeeding information is brought to Oedipus from Teiresias, from Thebes, somewhere away from the palace. The next witness comes from right within the palace: Jocasta at the center of the play and at the center of the issue arrives appropriately from the central doorway. The second half of the play brings messengers from outside again, rounding off the pattern. The messenger is from Corinth and the Shepherd from the hills. The progression is almost symmetrical. (One assumes that the messenger, however, came from a greater distance than the shepherd did.) But the point is that the stage provides a progression that is balanced, not only aesthetically but visually, for the balance is at the heart of the play's meaning. The entrances of the characters who are forces in accomplishing the fall of Oedipus are orderly and measurable visual changes. Sophocles' use of the stage is rhythmic and significant.

A single set then tends to be rhythmic (1) in that it operates like a painting or sculpture, making us aware of a recurrence of elements, of an alternation between stable and free elements, and of a progression which stimulates attention, and (2) in that it serves as a kind of repetition in itself which gives form to changes that happen upon it, indicating meaning through the nature of those changes.

Many playwrights of realism and its rebellious offspring (theatricalism, formalism, absurdism) have written plays for a single scene. Strindberg explains in his "Preface to *Miss Julie*" that the single setting was a conscious and purposeful choice for him. He hoped to achieve a more realistic effect by blending the characters and the all-important environment, and he wished to discourage the use of elaborate, extravagant, nonrealistic scenery.[3] Practical considerations mixed with aesthetic ones may be at the heart of many a playwright's choice of a single setting, so that one wonders to what extent the playwright has chosen on the basis of aesthetics. But just as the playwright of ancient Greece had many decisions already made for him by society and by theatrical tradition, so playwrights of all periods are dealt "limitations" of some sort. They may or may not love those limitations, but it is the inspiration born of them—the use of scenic conventions for meaning—that is the telling factor.

Strindberg's use of the single scene for *The Father* is particularly interesting. It illustrates the potential for a rhythmic, therefore symbolic, scenic background in a primarily realistic play. Certain of his symbols are in some ways decorative. They serve as reminders of the action of the play. The scene Strindberg describes is masculine in feeling. It holds the Captain's weapons, reading materials and arms, for he is, in a manner of speaking, a scholar and a soldier. And it holds symbols of ongoing life, a clock and a burning lamp. These are to act as a comment on his fall. The weapons comment on the Captain's impotence, the reading materials speak of his strengths, the clock continues to mark time as he dies. The constant presence of the burning lamp mocks him. Here is Strindberg's description of the scene for acts 1, 2, and 3. It is the manner in which the scene "repeats" in succeeding acts that provides the major rhythmic effect.

> The sitting-room at the CAPTAIN's. There is a door a little to the right at the back. In the middle of the room, a large round table stewn with newspapers and magazines. To right a leather covered sofa and table. In the right-hand corner a private door. At left there is a door leading to the inner room and a desk with a clock on it. Game-bags, guns and other arms hang on the walls. Army coats hang near door at back. On the large table stands a lighted lamp.

> The same scene as the previous act. A lighted lamp is on the table; it is night.

> Same scene. Another lamp on the table. The private door is barricaded with a chair.[4]

It is a great challenge to a director and designer to translate the rhythm of the printed description of a scene into a visual reality. The visual rhythm Strindberg demands here is: many things of interest, focus somewhat on lamp; sharper focus on lamp; focus on lamp.

With what effect does the room narrow to a lighted lamp? In the war between the sexes that *The Father* describes, the Captain (Adolph) tries to fight for his reason with his reason. He is first concerned with his daughter Berta's future, but the battle takes on cosmic proportions as he and his wife Laura fight a battle of wills. The Captain's intelligence is pitted against Laura's instinctual energy until his major strength, his mind, begins to fall to pieces. He resorts to all sorts of weapons to defend himself, but all weapons only mock him. The Captain's intelligence is his weapon in the first half of the play. Laura uses his theories and his very words against him. The lamp becomes a weapon in act 2. It burns on through the middle of the night. In a sense, it comes to represent Laura's staggering reserves of energy and persistence. Adolph throws the lighted lamp in Laura's face. She gets out of the way in time, but she also uses the fact that he threw the lamp as proof of insanity. His weapon is used against him, again. The gun, a more traditional weapon, is aimed by the Captain at his own daughter, Berta, in act 3. But the cartridges have been removed at Laura's command. Again he is mocked by a weapon. If anyone can be considered a victor in this deadly battle, Laura is winning. The new lamp which burns through act 3 is a constant irony, for it reminds us that in hurling a lamp at Laura, the Captain was simply spending his fury at something that could not be destroyed.

Throughout all these changes, through the Captain's fall, the visual scene remains the same. In a sense it repeats itself. The Captain uses several of the properties that have become symbols as the play progresses, all of them with no success. And Strindberg accents one ironic change: Laura replaces the broken lamp with another, and she too goes on, negating all of the Captain's acts by using them against him. The repetition of the visual scene, with its one major change, tells the story in symbolic, visual terms. Progression in this case is the product of repetition with one major change.

Henrik Ibsen used a single scene in some of his plays. *Ghosts* and *Hedda Gabler* are excellent examples of the rhythm of a single scene. Ibsen makes us aware in each case of what the room represents, who or what changes it, and what the change means. Irony is the keynote in Ibsen's use of settings. Even though Francis Fergusson says a good deal that is illuminating about *Ghosts* in his essay, "The Tragic Rhythm in a Small Figure," he seems to overstate the case for the supportive rather than the ironic functions of the set Ibsen describes. Fergusson describes the scene as a blank photograph in the following passage: "As Ibsen was fighting to present his poetic vision within the narrow theatre admitted by modern realism, so his protagonist Mrs. Alving is fighting to realize her sense of human life in the blank photograph of her own stuffy parlor. She discovers there no means, no terms, and no nourishment; that is the truncated tragedy which underlies the savage thesis of the play."[5] Fergusson, then, sees the set as representative of what really constitutes Mrs. Alving's existence, a blank photograph, an image of life. Ibsen's words suggest a more ironic image. William Archer translates Ibsen's own description as follows:

> A spacious garden-room, with one door to the left, and two doors to the right. In the middle of the room a round table, with chairs about it. On the table lie books, periodicals, and newspapers. In the foreground to the left a window, and by it a small sofa, with a worktable in front of it. In the background, the room is continued into a somewhat narrower conservatory, the walls of which are formed by large panes of glass. In the right-hand wall of the conservatory is a door leading down into the garden. Through the glass wall a gloomy fjord-landscape is faintly visible, veiled by steady rain.
>
> (P. 15)

Ibsen describes the room as spacious, a feeling which would be enhanced by the windows and walls of glass. In terms of stability and freedom in visual design, the set as he writes of it provides a good deal of free space. Ibsen's image seems more ironic because it describes the public image or facade of Mrs. Alving's life. To the community she attempts to give an impression of ordered well-being. In Ibsen's words, a gloomy fjord-landscape is visible, veiled by a steady rain. Yet Fergusson refers to the scene in terms of a cramped interior and an exhilarating wilderness: "Ibsen always felt this exhilarating wilderness behind his cramped interiors."[6] Where Ibsen is ironic, Fergusson seems to see him as straightforward. Where Ibsen is more straightforward about his visual symbolism, Fergusson sees him as ironic. It seems more appropriate to see the scene in Ibsen's terms: the gloom comes from without, darkening a room which, for all appearances, is conventional, spacious, and pleasant.[7]

Interpretations aside for the moment, the fact remains that Ibsen has chosen to show us an ordered place that is Mrs. Alving's parlor. It is a stage space, a representation of a room which may be changed by human forces from within the room, by human forces beyond the room (in other rooms, and outside the house), and by forces of nature, even more removed. As Mrs. Alving fights for the light or truth of her human condition, Ibsen works changes on the stable scene, changes that represent the shaking of the status quo. He uses two images to comment upon her search: the nonvisual image of the light of information and the visual image of the light of fire. Both work changes upon the stability of the scene and both are related. Mrs. Alving's room—and her life—are being bombarded by the truth, which, in classical fashion, seems to emerge in all its destructiveness in one day.

Not to be minimized are the many places from which other characters come into Mrs. Alving's living room and into her life. Each brings a little more of the past and a little more of the truth to the fore. Engstrand, carpenter and clubfoot, enters from the garden. He makes us wonder early in the play just what his relationship to Regina and the rest of the household is. Manders enters from without, from society, and his self-righteousness spurs Mrs. Alving to reveal some of the truth. Voices from the dining room force her to unmask even more of the truth. Meanwhile Oswald's appearance, looking like his father, is a broad hint that the past is encroaching. The entrance of each character in act 1 gives the progressive sense of the past moving in on the present, from every side, from without and within.

The physical look of the set changes three important times in act 2. Oswald has just complained to his mother that darkness shrouds their home: "I can't set to work at anything. . . . In such weather as this? Without a single ray of sunshine the whole day?" (p. 30). And he is just about to tell his mother that he is ill.

His illness, of course, is at the center of the play's meaning. The source of his disease was the "joy of life of his father"; the revelation of it will eventually constitute the final "light" of truth to Mrs. Alving; one of the specific forms of it is blindness. Just as Oswald begins to tell his mother that he is ill, Ibsen asks for a change of the scene with light: "*A silence. Twilight slowly begins to fall. OSWALD paces to and fro across the room*" (p. 30). Moments later he tells his mother what is wrong with him, and even though she understands something of the cause, she cannot make up her mind to tell him. Oswald is forcing the truth or light on her just as the universe is forcing darkness upon her. The following is an important passage.

OSWALD. . . . And then—it's so dark here! *(MRS. ALVING pulls a bell-rope on the right)* And this ceaseless rain! It may go on week after week, for months together. Never to get a glimpse of the sun! I can't recollect ever having seen the sun shine all the times I've been at home. . . .

MRS. ALVING. . . . Let us have the lamp in. (Pp. 31–32)

Later in act 2, just as Mrs. Alving has decided that yet another truth must be handled—that Regina is really Oswald's half-sister—she finds that the moment of truth must be delayed. Oswald shouts, "Where does that light come from?" and Regina answers, "The Orphanage is on fire!" (p. 34). And so, the changing light on the stage not only changes moods and tones, which in itself is an important contribution; but it also comments ironically upon the search for the truth which is associated with the light.

In act 3 the orphanage is, we are told, still burning. "*There is only a faint glow from the conflagration*" (p. 34). Mrs. Alving finally tells the story she had intended to tell, and Regina leaves as a result. The only light in the room is the lamp that Regina brought in in act 2, just as Mrs. Alving was trying to come to grips with Oswald's description of his illness. It is after Regina leaves that Oswald tells his mother the remainder of the truth about his condition—that it will affect his brain in such a way that it will make him a helpless child again. Since he refuses to endure such a living out of his life, he wrings from his mother the promise that she will administer morphia tablets should such a course of action become necessary. At this point, *"Day is breaking. The lamp is still burning on the table"* (p. 39). Mrs. Alving is unable to believe the worst of the truth or of the universe that controls her world. She fights for some view of life as still manageable and still controllable in spite of all its horrors.

MRS. ALVING. . . . There now. The crisis is over. You see how easily it passed! Oh, I was sure it would.—And do you see, Oswald, what a lovely day we are going to have? Brilliant sunshine! Now you can really see your home.
    (She goes to the table and puts out the lamp. Sunrise. The glacier and the snow-peaks in the background glow in the morning light.)
OSWALD *(sits in the arm-chair with his back towards the landscape, without moving. Suddenly he says:)* Mother, give me the sun.
MRS. ALVING. . . . What do you say?
OSWALD *(repeats in a dull, toneless voice).* The sun. The sun.   (P. 39)

The light from outside blazes as Oswald repeatedly asks for the sun. It shines upon him at just the moment he has become incapable of seeing it.

    Ibsen is the master of visual symbol and visual irony. His single scene for *Ghosts* changes rhythmically in two ways. First, as each character enters, we see that some new truth is brought to light by forces from all sides, all directions, all stratas of society. The single room gives us the sense that forces are moving in upon the room. Second, and more important, the room changes subtly as Mrs. Alving struggles with the truth. The changing light comments upon her actions and the potential effectiveness of them. We watch her call for lamps and snuff them out. But she is a puppet of the universe. Her acts are controlled by nature. The fate which nature represents in this play is a savage and unrelenting force.

    Light is a rhythmic and repetitive element of the visual drama of *Ghosts*. It is the factor that changes the stable scene. It is a small thing in itself and is easily motivated as realistic detail in a play of this style. But there is an important progression to the changes, and since the light is *the* major change in what otherwise remains stable, it is an extremely important change. The progression is as follows. In act 1 "the universe" provides meager, general light through the rain. In acts 2 and 3 Mrs. Alving controls the light to provide relief from the gloom of night. And she appears to be in control. But she cannot control the light of the orphanage fire or the light of the sun. And since all light is a property of fire or burning of some sort, of destruction of something, it is an appropriate ironic symbol. Each time light is used in the play, it seems like a good thing, it is certainly necessary, but it always spells some sort of destruction. Something is destroyed each time light burns in *Ghosts*.

Ibsen uses a complex network of symbols in *Ghosts* of which light is only one. A full understanding of the play is dependent upon an understanding of how the symbolic references relate to each other: father figures, disease, inheritance, the orphanage, the brothel, Engstrand's game leg, Captain Alving's pipe, religion, "Pastor," the sun—among others. It is a considerable disservice to Ibsen, because he uses such a complex network of symbols, to isolate one symbol from the rest. But it is a necessary disservice if we are to focus an examination on the rhythm of a single scene. Scenic rhythm, like dialogue rhythm, is inextricably bound to all other elements of the play. The method for the moment, however, is investigation by isolation, in hopes of a better understanding of the nature and complexity of rhythm. Ibsen, having been done a disservice once, is perhaps somewhat immune to the blows.

In *Hedda Gabler* Ibsen uses the single scene again. And again it is anything but static. The significant "changes" come less from the universe and more from the human forces in this play than in *Ghosts*. It is Hedda who is constantly changing the place. Again, the changes are small and realistically motivated, but they are at the same time providing a rhythm of change and pointing a symbolic progression. Hedda first changes the room by shutting out the light when others are around and letting it in again when she is alone. (Light and fire are used to some extent symbolically as they are in *Ghosts* and, for that matter, in most of Ibsen's plays.) The light of fire is used as Hedda burns the manuscript which Lövborg and Thea have created.

It seems as though someone is always crossing Hedda unintentionally. Aunt Juliana opens the doors in act 1. Berta is forever bringing in a lighted lamp. But Ibsen has written one important major physical change. And this time Hedda is "crossed" too. Hedda changes the furniture around: she moves her old piano to another room and replaces it with an elegant writing table. The piano room becomes her refuge when she is desperate. She eventually kills herself there. The little writing table, her elegant touch to the room, holds the pistol with which she destroys Lövborg (and by circumstance herself). It is also the spot Tesman and Thea choose to reconstruct the work of Eilert Lövborg. Each physical change of the scene that Hedda makes or each acceptance of the place as it is (she wanders about in the dark in act 4) is only reversed, either by Hedda or by someone else who is oblivious to her desires or intentions. The visual drama in the changes made upon the single scene support the meaning of the play. Hedda is a prisoner in a conventionally handsome arrangement. Every change she tries to make only imprisons her more. It is ironic that her very acts should be used against her. She destroys Eilert's manuscript, but it will be born again. She destroys Eilert for many reasons, but she destroys him—the potential love interest—only to be faced with Brack and a far more demeaning situation. She tries to destroy Thea because Thea has a talent for inspiring others and "creating" new life in others, only to watch Thea inspire Tesman. So it is appropriate that Hedda's selfish and dissatisfied change of furniture should provide the ironic tableau of the play.

The visual scene is always a metaphor for the drama to some extent. Many times changes in the scene are minimal, apparently careless, and likely to go unnoticed by an audience. But the audience is not likely to be unaffected by the progression of changes. They have probably come to accept the stability of the single scene without thinking about it, but it constantly provides a repetition upon which changes, when worked, point to a progression.

Even in so light a play as *Hay Fever*, the scene echoes the play and moves the action rhythmically. Coward does not go into detail about the look of the stage, but from his brief descriptions and stage directions, we get the following progression: A living room extremely comfortable and extremely untidy. It is lived in and looks like a family room. It does not look like a room about to receive four relative strangers as guests. It proves itself a family room as we watch the Bliss family draw, read, argue, and flop about on the comfortable furniture. When we find out that guests (four of them) are arriving, we must square this information with what we see. There is no massive tidying of the place. If, in a production there is any at all, it would likely give the impression that it is careless and coincidental. It is not written in. Except for the addition of flowers, the place remains the same for the arrival of the guests. When the guests have all arrived, the only change in the room is the arrival of a tea cart. But the tea is served badly, and act 1 ends with a room full of uncomfortable people as it begins to rain. In act 2 the room looks the same. The rain, however, has apparently ceased. And the family has rallied enough to put drinks out. But when David informs Myra that there isn't any ice, we are not quite certain that there ever was any. Act 3 affords the biggest change of all. The family room has become a breakfast room. The breakfast things are laid out, but the family is nowhere about. There are no hosts for the guests, we are told the food is bad, and it is now pouring. The guests and the family eat in separate shifts.

How is the single scene rhythmic in *Hay Fever*? The place changes little except that in each act the amenities with regard to refreshment are observed in a poor and haphazard manner. As the guests are served tea, they are provided with little sustenance in the way of hostlike conversation. As they are served drinks, they are overwhelmed with aggressive conversation which has little or nothing to do with them. As they *serve themselves* breakfast, they must talk to each other, for none of the Blisses appear. Their physical absence emphasizes their absence in spirit in the earlier acts. As is usual with rhythmic patterns, something remains stable, something changes (the amenities and the attempts at politeness by the Blisses) pointing to a final progression. In this case, the final point of the progression is the separation of both camps. The guests leave the family to themselves by sneaking out of the house after breakfast to make a speedy return to London.

Samuel Beckett has a habit, too, of changing the minimal to point his progressions, but he does so in a tone and with an intent quite different from the playwrights discussed so far. His physical scenes, like his plays, are so pared down to the bones of meaning that nothing can be taken as accidental, even by the most naive reader or playgoer. We are forced into awareness of the fact that his visual image is a metaphor for the meaning of the play. He creates in *Waiting for Godot* the simplest sort of visual rhythm, but it, like his dialogue, is full of meaning.

In *Waiting for Godot* he asks for *"A country road. A tree. Evening"* (p. 6). He writes that Estragon is sitting on a low mound. The tree and the mound are the only solid things on a barren landscape. The tree and the mound echo Vladimir and Estragon, and the tramps echo the landscape. Vladimir, the stage directions indicate, is standing more often than not, vertical in a sense like the tree. Estragon sees "the tree" as more of a bush, but it is upright nevertheless. Estragon uses the mound more often than Vladimir does—to sit on, to recline on, to sleep upon. Pozzo, interestingly, comes equipped with his own stool. Lucky stands. If these pared down visual cues are not to be taken seriously, why do they keep repeating their echoes throughout the play? Vladimir, the optimist, the aggressor, the thinker, the standing figure, has trouble with his hat. Estragon, the passive, the grounded, the more sensual figure, has trouble with his boots. This echo, like the "up" and "down" words of their dialogue is repeated a number of times. For instance, just before

Pozzo's "falling night" speech of act 1, "ESTRAGON *is fiddling with his boot again*, VLADIMIR *with his hat.*"

As they continue to fiddle, Pozzo, irritated, cracks his whip. "LUCKY *jumps*. VLADIMIR's *hat*, ESTRAGON 's *boot*, LUCKY's *hat, fall to the ground*" (pp. 24–25). That brief moment of burlesque calls attention not only to the tramps and their symbolic costume pieces, but also to the fact that Lucky and Vladimir reacted in much the same way. Do the tree and the mound figure in any such pattern? Both those solid elements of the set, the only masses in the void, *must* figure in the action of the play if it is to be any more theatrical than a dramatic reading. Both are used in an important manner at the end of act 1 as Vladimir and Estragon play out their repeated conflict between hope and despair, activity and passivity, belief and cynicism. Vladimir keeps pulling Estragon after him. Note the progression from both tramps up to both tramps down on the mound.

VLADIMIR. Are you mad? We must take cover. *(He takes* ESTRAGON *by the arm.)* Come on. *(He draws* ESTRAGON *after him.* ESTRAGON *yields, then resists. They halt.)*
ESTRAGON *(looking at the tree).* Pity we haven't got a bit of rope.
VLADIMIR. Come on. It's cold.
    (He draws ESTRAGON *after him. As before.)*
ESTRAGON. Remind me to bring a bit of rope to-morrow.
VLADIMIR. Yes. Come on.
    (He draws him after him. As before.) (P. 35)

The stage direction repeats word for word several lines later, so that the repeated pulling and resisting is itself rhythmic. It happens three times in quick succession in the exchange quoted above, is interrupted by an exchange which takes about the same amount of time as the three pantomimes have taken, and the pantomime is repeated once again. Then Estragon phrases his resistance and the tide of their decision is turned. Estragon gets Vladimir down.

ESTRAGON. Wait!
VLADIMIR. I'm cold!

ESTRAGON. Wait! *(He moves away from* VLADIMIR.*)* I sometimes wonder
    if we wouldn't have been better off alone, each one for himself. *(He
    crosses the stage and sits down on the mound.)* We weren't made for
    the same road.
VLADIMIR *(without anger)*. It's not certain.
ESTRAGON. No, nothing is certain.
    *(*VLADIMIR *slowly crosses the stage and sits down beside* ESTRAGON.*)*
VLADIMIR. We can still part, if you think it would be better.
ESTRAGON. It's not worth while now.
    (Silence.)
VLADIMIR. No, it's not worth while now.
    (Silence.)
ESTRAGON. Well, shall we go?
VLADIMIR. Yes, let's go.
    (They do not move.)   (P. 35)

If Beckett is fond of a progression in which change only gives
way to sameness, he is also fond of the "minimal progression."
His changes are as pared down as are his sets and his dialogue.
The description of act 2 is as follows: *"Next day. Same time.
Same place"* (p. 36). Even the brevity of the description implies a
visual rhythm. But there are *some* changes. Estragon's boots
are there, but not Estragon. (Estragon and his boots, but no Vladimir, was the opening image of act 1.) Lucky's hat remains in
the same place. *"The tree has four or five leaves"* (p. 37). The
tree has leaves, just enough of them to tell us it is alive. Should
that fact be taken seriously? It is an image of minimal life and of
hope. It is also an image of minimal change. Vladimir sings in
this act. He also thinks more, or at any rate, expresses his
thoughts more. He inherits Lucky's hat. An interesting moment
in act 2 is Vladimir's coaching Estragon to hide so he won't be
beaten.

VLADIMIR. . . . Your only hope left is to disappear.
ESTRAGON. Where?
VLADIMIR. Behind the tree. *(*ESTRAGON *hesitates.)* Quick! Behind the tree.
    *(*ESTRAGON *goes and crouches behind the tree, realizes he is not hid-*

den, comes out from behind the tree.) Decidedly this tree will not have been the slightest use to us. (Pp. 47–48)

When the tramps do their exercises, Vladimir insists on Estragon's doing "the tree," which he does first to demonstrate. It consists of staggering about on one leg, an appropriate image of Vladimir's strategy—upright, but very shaky and liable to fall at any moment. Estragon *"staggers worse"* (p. 49). Just then, Pozzo and Lucky enter, and in something of a reversal of the first Pozzo-Lucky scene, all four spend quite a bit of time on the ground. Beckett's tremendous care in making explicit his ideas is some indication that he did not take any of his pared-down details lightly and intended that we notice them for their symbolic contributions. Whether he did so consciously or not is another matter and of no real significance here. His careful detail is consistently important.

The end of the second act is often described as exactly like the end of the first. It is not quite the same, and again, Beckett's careful detail should be examined. Vladimir does not drag Estragon. In fact, Estragon drags Vladimir to the tree to contemplate it and discuss again their chances of hanging themselves. The tree is not the problem this time. The problem is the faulty rope that holds up Estragon's trousers. Vladimir is still having trouble with his hat, although it is Lucky's hat. The tramps do not sit down. They freeze in a standing position this time. The correct balance, really, considering that all changes are for the worst, is that they should end "up."

I do not mean to imply any one-to-one relationship between Vladimir and the tree and Estragon and the mound. The scene simply echoes the two dominant postures of man.

The scenic rhythm, so simple, is also extremely complex. It has been impossible, for instance, to discuss it without at least a mention of some of the other patterns it relates to. A mound–a tree–and void–nearly night progresses to a mound–a tree–and void–nearly night—except that the tree has a few leaves. A more cruelly comic Tantalus image is hard to find, except in other works of Beckett. Those few leaves mock reality, but they support the "going on" with it that we sense at the end of the play. The presence of a few leaves does not quite balance with hope the awful vision of a fallen Pozzo and Lucky, but it keeps the scales from tipping totally to despair. Those few leaves say to the tramps that although almost everything is the same, or worse, something is different, which means that there must be life somewhere.

Beckett uses much the same kind of progression in his *Happy Days;* scorched grass and void surround a mound in which Winnie is buried to the waist. The first visual image to meet our eyes is that of a woman halfway in her grave. The action of the play is ironic to say the least. Winnie, halfway in her grave, still has, in a literal sense, lots of little things to keep her going. She has a toothbrush, but she is running out of toothpaste; a tonic for "loss of spirits,"[8] but she takes the final dose early in the play; spectacles, a mirror, and a hat, all of which serve her, but not particularly well; a gun, which provides insurance for the future; and a parasol, her only protection, which burns. The loss of the parasol provokes nothing more violent from Winnie than "Ah earth you old extinguisher" (p. 37), which gives rise to a philosophical and quite rhetorical speech on the blazing of the sun and what it could do to her. Winnie's "little things" balance her half-buried condition and physically represent her attempts to "go on with it." And she has little things of another sort, even more important to her. Willie directs a few comments to her. He holds up his hand to indicate that he is listening. He even answers a question or two.

Act 2 provides repetition of the same with changes. Winnie is still buried, of course, but now more deeply—to her neck. She cannot use her bag, her parasol, her revolver which mocks her with its nearness. The little things which carry her through the day are now all abstract things. She cannot see or hear Willie, but she considers that a blessing, because not *knowing* whether he is there or not makes it possible for her to imagine and hope.

It is "a mercy." Beckett's rhythmic progression points to a strained balance as it did in *Waiting for Godot*. For everything that is *so much worse*, Winnie manages to find something to make existence *a little better*. For instance, she can still open and close her eyes which is a source of pleasure to her. Beckett's progression includes another Tantalus image. Winnie's bag, parasol, and gun are all there, but she cannot use them. Willie finally emerges at the end of act 2, looking better and more fit than usual, but she cannot touch him. He speaks only one word now—"Win"—when she could use a few more. And his garb is ambiguous. Does his dressing up mean that he wants to please her and that he has chosen the worst possible moment to become motivated? Or has he perhaps chosen the best? Or does it mean that he is going away, leaving Winnie to make the best of absolutely nothing? The answer is not important really. The ambiguity is. The scenic progression alone has told us that although the "big foot" from on high keeps pressing Winnie (and us by extension) further and further into the ground, she is left with just enough of her senses to be tempted by life. Even though she can see the means of life and death just out of reach and mocking her, Winnie, representing all of us, has a limitless power, it seems, of going on, of investing each word, object, thought, and memory that is left to her with symbolic meaning.

Beckett's use of the single scene is masterful. As in *Waiting for Godot*, the scene of *Happy Days* says a great deal. The scene shows us that the only solid thing is the earth. The rest is space or void. Yet the void becomes a "stable" element in one sense because nothing concrete intrudes to change it. We are either paralyzed by the earth and unable to act or move (Winnie) or paralyzed by the void and unable to or unwilling to speak (Willie). Again Beckett's set echoes the images of the characters and provides progression, minimal progression, but maximal use of the progression.

A single scene, then, serves as a form of repetition for the whole play. Generally it does so by representing or standing for something. Yet always, no matter how simple the single scene is, there is some progression either in its use or in the change of some few elements in what otherwise remains stable. In its most static form (alone, and prior to curtain, for instance) a scene operates like a painting, and like a painting it is rhythmic in its repeated and alternating elements, in its logical group-ings, in its lines or directions which force our eyes to make a rhythmic sweep of the stage. The scene is a rhythmic part of the whole play because it echoes the progression of the action; or because it mirrors the progression of the action in reverse, pro-viding counterpoint; or because it does both, providing irony.

The Polyscenic Stage

Playwrights who do not see their plays as a single scene write their visual effects with one of several schemes for a changing scene. The rhythmic potential of a changing scene is great. There are however, three basic manners of representing multiple scenes, and their effects are obviously somewhat different from each other. They are: (1) the polyscenic stage of juxtaposition used primarily by the medieval and modern playwright; (2) the panoramic approach, used by medieval, Renaissance, Restoration, and modern playwrights (for example, Jarry in his *Ubu* plays, the expressionists, and Bertolt Brecht in his epic dramas); and (3) the limited progression used primarily by the realistic and naturalistic playwrights. In the polyscenic approach, anywhere from two to many scenes are shown simultaneously; in the panoramic approach, many places are shown successively; in the limited change, of course, fewer places (generally two to four) are shown successively. Panoramic and limited progressions will be dealt with later, after an examination of the rhythm of the polyscenic approach.

The mystery cycles of Europe were performed on stages of all sorts from earthen arenas to marketplaces to pageant wagons. No matter what the space for the performance, certain basic ideas and methodologies predominated across country lines. The cycles were comprised of many one-act plays, and each play demanded one or more specific "places." Places of the earth were indicated by "mansions" (or loci), structures of partially symbolic, partially realistic design. These mansions, many or few (perhaps even in some cases one at a time), were placed on a *platea*, a neutral playing area representing all of the known earth. Two mansions, in addition to earthly locales, appeared at some point in nearly every cycle. These were the structures representing heaven and hell. Available sources indicate that heaven and hell were placed in stationary productions at least in such a way as to flank the earth from opposite sides or from above and below.

No matter how many times the scene changed in a cycle, the idea was repeated that there were many structures on earth and that heaven and hell were the important weights on either side. There is rhythmic balance in just the idea of the scenic representation: sameness in that mansions represent all places; difference in that two places flank the rest and hold special significance for the audience. Glynne Wickham describes the rhythmic balance in aesthetic terms:

The Mediaeval "stage-designer" was faced with the same basic problem that confronts his counterpart today: to provide upon the stage a convincing representation of the Universe as understood by his audience. To the spectator of the Middle Ages, the Universe consisted of three separate but interrelated worlds—Heaven, Earth and Hell—all three equally real. Heaven and Hell were interpreted in terms of the known world of Earth. The only differences of importance for the stage-designer were that Heaven lacked all the blemishes of Earth while Hell exaggerated those blemishes to the exclusion of all else.[1]

When the cycles were given a stationary performance, the relationship between scenes could be emphasized. The stage could present visual ironies based upon such questions as: What scenes are *close* to hell? Or heaven? Does mankind seem to be progressing toward heaven or hell? What is happening in one place while something is occurring in another? Value judgments could be emphasized by the placement of a single scene. Progression could be emphasized by the direction of action from scene to scene. Visual irony could be emphasized by simultaneous action. Stable was the structure of the universe. Flexible was the journey of a human being, or the human race, through the universe.

Controversy continues about how consistently pageant wagons were used, what they actually looked like, how many mansions appeared on any one wagon, whether several wagons joined together for a performance, and whether each wagon had an "above" and a "below" to represent heaven and hell. It is not the province of this study to deal with the controversies, but merely to point out that in spite of them we can still make some conclusions about the rhythm of the polyscenic stage, which, nobody argues, existed much of the time. In any case, juxtaposition of scenes, with many places shown and an emphasis on progression, was a constant. The story of mankind's spiritual history was not a static story. And even when wagons were used, there was likely some insistent reminder—either heaven and hell mansions or places for heaven and hell on each wagon—of the two possible destinations at the end of the human journey.

In what is probably the best-known medieval mystery play, the anonymous master of Wakefield shows us visually a balance between a lowly, common mortal and the family of God. Mak is a thief; his wife, Gil, is an irritable fishwife, given to the bottle. In *The Second Shepherds' Play*, comic irony is the keynote when Mak steals a sheep from his friends who are shepherds, and he and Gil wrap it in swaddling clothes and call it a child to avoid being caught. The tone of the play remains comic, particularly when the birth hoax is discovered by the shepherds, and they toss Mak in a blanket as he pleads for mercy. The play might even be considered "finished" by some at this point since the action has progressed neatly from "sin" to repentance to forgiveness. The Wakefield master is a far more complex playwright, however, than such a progression would label him. He not only moves the action of the play back and forth from Mak's house (a place of comic deceit) and the fields, but he moves the final action of the play from the fields to the manger, a place where salvation is represented simply and awesomely at once. The two mansions not only represent places respectively closer to hell and heaven, with the shepherds traveling to both, but the poles of the action are represented visually by the two loci or places. Repetition occurs in that the shepherds take gifts to both "babies." Varied (and ironic) repetition occurs in that the first child is really a lamb disguised as a child, and the second is a child who will be known metaphorically as a lamb. Change occurs too in that the house of Mak is barred to the shepherds while the house of Christ is open to them. Progression occurs in that the shepherds move from the fields to a place where they are tried by deceit and from the fields (neutral ground, again) to a place where they are offered salvation.

Rhythmically the change of "place" emphasizes the journey of man through life to the alternatives of salvation or damnation. The alternation between the fields and Mak's house occupies over four-fifths of the play's stage time. The alternation between the fields and the manger makes up less than one-fifth the stage time. Yet the last is the important journey of life, the reward for other journeys traveled.

The polyscenic stage sets up the materials of its rhythm and executes rhythmic change by repeating the use of places, by repeating journeys from place to place, by providing visual irony (i.e., showing the relationships between places), and by emphasizing progression. The Wakefield master got a great deal of mileage out of juxtaposed scenes and the rhythmic balance afforded by dual action. Indeed Martial Rose, who feels that the Wakefield plays must have been given a stationary performance with a multiple set, indicates, by way of pursuing his argument, the manner in which rhythmic balance through simultaneous viewing of places was used by the master of Wakefield to underline irony and to literalize progression, even between plays:

The journey motif is best exemplified in *The Second Shepherds' Play* and *The Offering of the Magi*. In the former Mak's house is opposed to the manger; the shepherds pass from one to the other and even sleep on the green (634) between the two mansions. *The Offering of the Magi* is similarly staged with Herod's palace replacing Mak's house; similarly, too, the kings sleep, but this time in a litter (590), between the two mansions.[2]

Rose also lists the probable places for performance of *The Conspiracy*. Note the repetition of Pilate's hall, journeying *(platea)*, and Mount Olivet (line numbers are in parentheses):

1. Pilate's hall (1-313)
2. Jesus and his disciples (314-333)
3. John and Peter on their way to Jerusalem, and
4. Their meeting with Paterfamilias outside his house (334-345)
5. The chamber of the Last Supper (strewn with rushes), the scene of the washing of feet (346-491)
6. The two levels of Olivet, one where Jesus prays and the other where the disciples sleep (492-599)
7. During which scene God appears in heaven's tower (528-555)
8. Pilate's hall (560-651)
9. From Olivet to the place of capture (652-707)
10. Pilate's hall (708-747)
11. Malcus and the soldiers lead Jesus to Caiaphas' hall (748-755)[3]

Rose concludes that "there is every indication dramatically that the capture is staged on ground level midway between Mount Olivet and Pilate's hall."[4] Such staging would emphasize appropriately the progression of the play—Jesus caught finally "between" Pilate and his own disciple, Judas. So it appears that even if a minimal number of scenes or places was shown for each play, the rhythm of the play took on the characteristics of the journey from place to place, and likely two places, representing the poles of the action took some sort of dominant positions in the dramatic action.

The polyscenic stage of juxtaposition is one of the rarer forms of scenic representation throughout theatre history. It seems to have gone out of fashion after the Middle Ages only to return occasionally in the contemporary theatre as a device for the pointing of visual irony, and visual irony over time is rhythm. Miller's *Death of a Salesman* moves us through parts of Willie's house, from the inside of the house to the outside world, and from the real world to the world of fantasies and dreams. His effect is irony in motion through all the "double images." By making us aware of two places at once, Miller is making us aware of two worlds of consciousness which do not and cannot meet.

Harold Pinter uses a somewhat abstract polyscenic stage in *A Slight Ache*. Although the play was originally written for radio, "place" and the conflict between symbolic places is interesting, indeed one of the joys of the play when it is staged. According to Pinter, symbolic scenery is to be used to represent locations. When Edward asks Flora to take him into the garden, *"they move from the study door to a chair under a canopy"* (p. 28). Edward finds it peaceful and he and Flora talk about the trees and birds, none of which we expect to *see* or *hear*. The action of the play spans four important places and shows us movement (or journeys) between them. Those places are a breakfast table, the scullery, Edward's study, and the garden. Pinter asks that the places be *"indicated with a minimum of scenery and props"* (p. 9). The most important climactic scenes take place in the study, Edward's territory. The scullery and the garden represent Flora's territory to a significant extent. The breakfast table is a somewhat neutral battleground for the opening of the play. When Edward appears in the scullery and in the garden, he is in Flora's territory. Fearful of the Matchseller throughout, Edward attempts to mask his fear with angry explosions, contemptuous mutterings, and cheerful chatter. When in his study, his fear is witnessed only by the ambiguous Matchseller. In the scullery and garden, it is witnessed by Flora. More important, perhaps, is that his fear is directly fed by Flora. Yet when Flora enters Edward's territory, the study, she is unruffled as always. She has invaded his hideout, his place of self-protection. And she takes it over by "adopting" the Matchseller, the representative of Edward's fear. It is appropriate that the play should end in Edward's study for the action of the drama is really a territorial battle of sorts. We finally see the victor taking possession of the land. Flora controls the study, the Matchseller, and Edward by the end.

A polyscenic stage operates rhythmically under the same principles which govern other manifestations of rhythm. It points to what is stable and what changes. For instance, we must be aware of Mak's house and its significance to understand the change to the manger, or at the very least to feel the rightness of the change. We must be aware that Pinter's stage space includes Edward's territory and Flora's territory before we can understand that Edward moves to Flora's territory for protection and Flora moves to Edward's territory for power. Too, we sense in each of the journeys that Edward resists Flora's territory even though he enters it, and that Flora is quite comfortable anywhere. We do not need to ask and answer questions consciously but we are provoked to ask certain kinds of questions by a polyscenic stage, such as, What do the shepherds go to Mak's house *for*? What does Edward go to the scullery *for*? We are made especially aware of the meaning of movement. A polyscenic stage gives us the distinct impression that all action takes place in a framework, that all movement takes place in a bounded universe, that there are several possible destinations of a progression, but not an infinite number. The poles for the action are representative and therefore come to take on symbolic meanings. As we watch progression from place to place, we watch the progression of irony. The pattern of a progression is its rhythm.

The Panoramic Stage

The Elizabethan stage was in many ways a variation of the medieval stage with its "heavens," earth, and cellarage. Renaissance plays, too, were outgrowths of medieval tradition. In a sense, the panoramic approach to staging is a variation on the polyscenic stage. The Renaissance stage of England, like the medieval stage, provokes a great deal of scholarly controversy over its staging conventions. But controversy aside, the few remaining facts of staging tell us the following: the stage could remind its audience of the structure of the Christian universe with the signs of the zodiac painted on the roof, the platform stage like a *platea* holding most of the action, and the space beneath the stage known as the dungeon, the cellarage, or hell. The stage also provided several entrance areas and acting areas: *something* represented an "above" for balcony scenes and the like; possibly something represented "within" for private scenes or so-called chamber scenes;[1] the space beneath the stage was known as "below," and although not an acting area, it was a possible entrance area, from which ghostly and otherworldly manifestations could emerge. Although in some of these respects (entrance places, for example) the Renaissance stage reminds us of the Greek stage, in more fundamental respects it is its very antithesis. Performance did not take place on a distanced, focused circle, but on a platform thrust into the midst of its audience. The Renaissance stage did not represent

134

one symbolic place, but many. The scenery was not wholly symbolic as we suspect the Greeks' was, but, according to the Rose Inventory, internal evidence of the plays, and the medieval tradition, was instead a curious combination of symbolic and realistic scenic devices. Such a combination is not really surprising or difficult to justify since every other aspect of the plays shows some combination of styles. The center of energy, as Frye notes, is somewhere between verse and prose. The subjects of the plays range from the sublime to the grotesque. The tone of many plays moves between tragedy and comedy.

The changes of subject, tone, and style are reflected in Elizabethan plays to some extent by changes of scene. Whatever actual scenery was used is not so important as the fact that the stage could and did encompass many places. They may simply have been represented by "exeunt" and "enter." But the places, like the hut of Mak and Gil or the manger, could represent qualities or forces which are balanced rhythmically throughout the play. The changes, moreover, tell us something about the progression of the play. Nevill Coghill points out that not only does Shakespeare provide us with mood changes and give us "comparisons" through a juxtaposition of scenes, but he creates a whole pattern in progression through a juxtaposition of "elements." He labels the elements in *Henry IV*, part 1, and finds the following pattern (which is quite rhythmic!) in operation:

Act I. Throne—Tavern—Rebels.
Act II. Tavern—Rebels—Tavern.
Act III. Rebels—Throne—Tavern.
Act IV. Rebels—Tavern—Rebels.
Act V. Throne—Rebels—BATTLE.[2]

It is interesting that the Ghost in *Hamlet* and the Witches in *Macbeth* first appear *outside* the respective palaces in Denmark and Scotland. When the Ghost and the supernatural manifestations in *Macbeth* move "indoors" we make some subconscious mental note that the damage to the protagonists' hopes of escape or survival is really complete.

An excellent model of the rhythm of a changing scene is Shakespeare's *Antony and Cleopatra*. The platform for this play holds many "places." The progression evolves not from simultaneous action or even from simultaneous viewing of the several "places" of the play, but from constant and regular changes from place to place. Much of the play takes place in or between Rome and Alexandria. Location ceases to be important in its own right after the action of the play is established because Rome and Alexandria come to represent the people and the forces that are in conflict throughout the play. Granville-Barker notes that Shakespeare "let the change of place speak through the identity of the characters and their action."[3] We tend to view the action (even if the only scenery is the characters who inhabit a place) as occurring on Caesar's ground or neutral ground or Cleopatra's ground, or in the ship scene, Pompey's "ground." No matter how many places are shown, the places represent stops along the way between two poles for the action: the rational, cold, warlike, aggressive world of Caesar and the emotional, impulsive, sensual, and somewhat lazy domain of Cleopatra.

Shakespeare is not content, needless to say, to invest the poles of conflict with simple meanings. Life in Alexandria is not without stress, for the hotheaded lovers guard each other jealously. When they argue, their arguments reach the proportions of a personal war, complete with intermediaries, negotiations, and so on. Life in Rome is not wholly emotionless, either. Caesar is capable at least of caring for Octavia. Similarities between war and love, between military slaughter and sex are only a part of the meaning of this complex play. A great part, but only a part, is characterized by betrayal themes. Those elements will be touched upon later, but suffice it to say that they are related to the subject of scenic rhythm. The subject of examination at this point is just that, the rhythm of the changes of scene—how Shakespeare has told the story of the play through the repetition and change of primarily visual elements (tied inextricably, of course, to dialogue).

Time in panoramic plays is an important concept in many ways. One of the ways, though, is the simple issue of how much time we spend in each place. In the case of *Antony and Cleopatra*, how much time do we spend in Rome, in Alexandria, on neutral ground—and in what order and with what effect do we spend that time? The repeated or recurring places are, as was previously mentioned, Rome and Egypt. No matter what simplicity or elaborateness marks the scenery, whether the places are indicated only by the characters who fill them, Rome and Egypt are the places to watch. Shakespeare starts us out in Egypt where the lovers enjoy "soft hours" and "wine enough." Rome intrudes repeatedly via letters for Antony. The play is to be a battle between Cleopatra the Lover and Caesar the Warrior for the life of Antony. Shakespeare, after having steeped us in Egypt, takes us to Rome for a briefer moment. Rome is without Antony, but Antony and Egypt are the subjects of Caesar's scene. In Egypt again, we see an Egypt without its Antony, and it is a pettier place without him.

Acts 2 and 3 are spent in and about Rome where war and politics dominate all discussions. Battles are planned, treaties are settled, a practical political marriage between Antony and Octavia is executed; treaties and marriage vows are also broken in short order. Shakespeare punctuates the Roman scenes with two important rhythmic variations. Twice he takes us back to Egypt where Cleopatra's abandon takes the form of "attacks" on the messenger who brings her word of Antony's marriage, and then manipulation of the same messenger. These comic scenes show us as well as remind us of the emotionalism and passion that differentiate Egypt from Rome. These switches of scene to Egypt function as strongly as any soothsaying and philosophizing can to tell us that Antony will be back in Egypt eventually, partly indeed because Shakespeare has made us want to see him there.

Shakespeare, always complex, never gives us quite what we are prepared to see. When we finally see Antony in Egypt again, with his Cleopatra again, they are talking war, not love.

From this point on (and it is about halfway through the play, the traditional crisis point), we know the lovers are doomed. In a literal sense the lovers' reconciliation means war with Caesar. In a metaphoric sense, Rome has affected Egypt. From midpoint onward the play takes place in Egypt or lands and seas nearby. Caesar is in Cleopatra's territory now; he is attacking her ground. He even moves, by deceit, his forces into her monument, the last place of protection.

Shakespeare's progression is not only a zigzagging back and forth between Rome and Egypt and between love and war, although both elements remain a part of the total dramatic experience of the play. His progression is also from peace to war and from the sensual to the aggressive. He starts us out in Egypt, the land of pleasure in the world of the play. Egypt's influence is eventually felt in Rome, carried there in a sense by Antony, for cold though Caesar is, the major events of the early scenes in Rome are reconciliation between Caesar and Antony, marriage, peace treaties with Pompey. The cold war is quite friendly. Pompey is a fair man when he refuses to be a butcher and insists on remaining a host. Word battles between Enobarbus and Agrippa are comic and friendly. Antony is flexible and good-natured much of the time. When Antony goes to Rome he takes a little of Egypt with him, and the war is "stopped" for the moment. Feasting, drinking, and joking mark the event. The progression reverses as the Rome principle begins to affect the action more and more. Caesar's and Antony's ways are not the same. Caesar has made war on Pompey and framed Lepidus. And when Antony returns to Egypt a little of Rome returns too. Egypt has a more warlike face. Harsh words are exchanged by the lovers. They go to war. And Caesar invades the territory and the monument.

Why is it rhythmically right that the play should resolve itself with Cleopatra and at Cleopatra's lodgings? Another visual rhythm prepares us for the final moments to a great extent, and that is the patterning of character entrances and exits which will be discussed later as the rhythm of symbolic gesture. It is through scene change, however, that we understand one major element of the progression of the action. The overall sweep of the play, its magnetic forces, become clear through the pattern of scene change. Rome is like a magnet which by repeated attempts draws Antony to itself. Egypt proves a stronger magnet yet, for not only is Antony drawn back, but so is Caesar and the Roman army, and with such force that they crash upon Egypt and destroy the lure itself.

The alternation of place describes one of the larger rhythmic patterns of *Antony and Cleopatra*. But there are progressions within progressions. Granville-Barker points out that one of Shakespeare's most masterly pieces of stagecraft may be found in the battle scenes of *Antony and Cleopatra*. The short scenes juxtaposed not only show the effect of three days' battle on the characters, but "give us a panorama of the entire event, since in its quick turns and confusions lie the significance of its tragedy."[4] Styan charts the progression in the somewhat cinematic act 4 battle scenes through the changing spirits of Antony: "up (iv), then down (v/vi), then up again (vii/viii), and then, more prolonged, in sober suspense (ix/xii). The audience's sense of war is thus constructed for the most part by its impressions of one man and one mind."[5]

Shakespeare, after investing places with meaning, begins to work countless ironies upon the established meanings. The multiscenic stage in Brecht's hands is generally used with considerably less complexity. Brecht would probably be the first to say so, and he would insist that he intended it that way. Since Shakespeare gets such a sense of movement from the changes in *Antony and Cleopatra* and since that movement works considerable emotional change upon an audience, Brecht would probably not find it objective enough. His flatter repetition of effects ensures the audience's awareness of the pattern of changes. Spanning twelve years and many cities and towns, the action of his *Mother Courage* illustrates the history of Anna

Fierling and her canteen through the Thirty Years' War. Repeating itself in almost every scene is the wagon that represents Mother Courage's livelihood. The wagon is the constant provoker of questions that Brecht has set up: Courage or commercialism? Wiliness or selfishness? Worldliness or stupidity? Brecht intends that Mother Courage's actions should be examined by an audience which does not take them as dramatic "musts." He tells a good deal of his story and poses a number of his questions through scenic change.

Brecht's changes are clearly rhythmic: places change from scene to scene; they are the free or flexible element of the progression. The wagon remains as the stable element. It appears in nearly every scene and when it is not actually visible, Brecht reminds us of it by giving Mother Courage actions like selling a capon (scene 2) or planning to file a complaint because her wagon was torn to ribbons (scene 4) or taking inventory inside a canteen tent (scene 6). It is interesting that every other scene for the first half of the play shows the wagon and every scene of the second half shows it. Whether we realize it or not it is becoming more of a constant. There is also an interesting progression of images of the wagon, the stable element from scene to scene. The wagon is an image that recurs with changes or variations. In scene 3 it has an ironically domestic touch: a clothesline stretches from the wagon to a cannon. This is the scene in which Mother Courage allows her son Swiss Cheese to die because she haggles over the price of his release for too long. The wagon stands in a war-ravaged village in scene 5, and we are told it stands outside a profitable canteen tent in scene 6. We see it being drawn along a highway in scene 7, drawn by Kattrin and Mother Courage who now *"wears a necklace of silver coins."* As for the wagon, *"new wares are hanging from it."*[6] The final ironic point in Brecht's progression occurs in scenes 11 and 12, in which *"the wagon, very far gone now, stands near a farmhouse with a straw roof"* (p. 103). This is the roof upon which Kattrin dies beating a drum to warn the town of imminent attack. The play's one moment of heroism is played with the wagon clearly in sight. After arranging Kattrin's burial, Mother Courage goes on pulling the wagon again.

The wagon repeats through all the changes of place, through all the actions imitated, but the changes or variations in its recurrence point to the ironic progression of the play. The scene changes tell us that the wagon continues to survive in good condition or bad, capitalizing on war and in spite of loss—just as its owner does.

The first impressions of a play with a changing scene in the panoramic style are somewhat different from those of a play with a polyscenic stage of juxtaposition. The spectator is made aware of change first and foremost, and later he attempts to find the stability or repetition in the changes. The world is seemingly unbounded, the possibilities seemingly infinite, and only in time, via repeated change, does the limited world of the play emerge and the finite number of possibilities present themselves. Repetition and change point to the balancing agents in a play, but they seem to be themselves balancing agents. Our lives would be orderless without repetition, and they would be monotonous beyond endurance without change. When we have too much of one-half the balance, we automatically seek the other. As spectators we do the same. When we are faced with change we attempt to order it, when we have ordered it we seek changes in the order (which we generally perceive by repetition). The panoramic plays of Shakespeare with their tremendously broad strokes of changes indicate a breadth and scope which is breathtaking. When the playwright has structured our experience so that we understand order and change at almost precisely the same moment, we are probably witnessing some manifestation of irony or paradox, the two building blocks of complex drama. It has been said that the better the playwright the more complexities per second exist in a play. That statement holds a great deal of truth, perhaps more than might be imagined at first. For each pattern of changes creates its own rhythmic force on a play, and where patterns overlap, in a seemingly chaotic, but ultimately orderly, pattern, we have complexity indeed. When jazz musicians overlap rhythms, pick them apart to show us how separate they are, and then put them back together again, they are doing something much like a playwright does in focusing our attention on separate elements of a play only to show later how they fit together.

The Limited Scenic Progression

Playwrights of the realistic and naturalistic genres often require two or more scenes for the playing out of their dramas. With Ibsen, Chekhov, or any of the masters for that matter, change of scene in a realistic play accomplishes much more than providing variety or scenic verisimilitude of "daily life."

In *The Master Builder*, a play with more poetic feeling than either *Ghosts* or *Hedda Gabler*, Ibsen moves his action and his master builder along a scenic path that comments ironically upon Solness' pathway to death. The progression is clear and linear—there is no doubling back on the journey, no repeat of place. Solness is on a death trip in which he sees youth as the scytheman pursuing him. He is described as the first man or the best in his profession and as a man who has been lucky in his climb to success. Solness is a firm believer in rhythmic balance. His luck makes him afraid, "for sooner or later the luck must turn, you see," he explains to Dr. Herdal in act 1. It will come from "the younger generation" (p. 237).

Solness' strategy for fighting defeat—not being the first man in his profession, the best builder, the highest on the tower—is to embrace his enemy, youth, to *adopt* youth in the person of Hilda. For once youth is on his side, he feels he can gain new power, new freedom, and most important, new youth for himself.

Ibsen, so fond of light as a symbol, uses light again in *The Master Builder*. He associates it with youth and freedom in gen-

143

eral, with Hilda in particular. His scenic progression tells the story of Solness' death trip in ironic terms. Solness moves progressively toward light, freedom, nature, and growth only to move closer to death. The first act takes place in Solness' workroom, a place removed from nature and unembellished with touches of nature. A desk, table and chairs, books and papers, and the reliable shaded lamps fill the work space. There are no images of freedom here. Moreover, descriptions of the three employees who also fill the space add to the sense of lifelessness. Knut Brovik is shrunken, his son Ragnar already has a slight stoop in his shoulders, Kaia is slender, delicate, and she wears a shade over her eyes. When Solness enters, his vigor provides a strong contrast to this faded atmosphere. Hilda will seem quite out of place in this workroom.

A sense of brightness and of ordered growth fills the act 2 scene, which Ibsen describes with quite a bit of attention to windows, glass, mirrors, the view, and the indoor plants. The outdoors and the indoors are combined in seeming harmony in this room. Images of freedom are ordered. Here is Ibsen's description:

> A prettily furnished small drawing-room in SOLNESS' house. In the back, a glass door leading out to the veranda and garden. The right-hand corner is cut off transversely by a large bay-window, in which are flower-stands. The left-hand corner is similarly cut off by a transverse wall, in which is a small door papered like the wall. On each side, an ordinary door. In front, on the right, a console table with a large mirror over it. Well-filled stands of plants and flowers. In front, on the left, a sofa with a table and chairs. Further back, a bookcase. Well forward in the room, before the bay window, a small table and some chairs. It is early in the day.   (P. 248)

Ibsen uses this room ironically. Mrs. Solness, who is supposed to have a gift for nurturing, goes about watering the plants. We find out later that she never goes into her own garden, where nature is wilder and not tamed as it is indoors.

Act 3 moves Solness outdoors toward a seeming lack of confinement. But confinement exists even outdoors in more subtle form. The veranda has a railing, the garden has a fence, the tower on the new house has a scaffold around it, and the evening sun is surrounded by clouds:

> The large, broad verandah of SOLNESS' dwelling-house. Part of the house, with outer door leading to the verandah, is seen to the left. A railing along the verandah to the right. At the back, from the end of the verandah, a flight of steps leads down to the garden below. Tall old trees in the garden spread their branches over the verandah and towards the house. Far to the right, in among the trees, a glimpse is caught of the lower part of the new villa, with scaffolding round so much as is seen of the tower. In the background the garden is bounded by an old wooden fence. Outside the fence, a street with low, tumble-down cottages.
> Evening sky with sun-lit clouds.   (P. 270)

The scene changes of *The Master Builder* poetically underline the play. Repeated are images of confinement. The changes are those of seemingly increasing freedom—more space, more growth, more comfort. The progression is from recognizable confinement to a mirage of freedom. The Master Builder seems to come closer and closer to freedom, only to die in the attempt. As he tries to own Hilda, youth, and freedom, the scene changes comment ironically upon just how much he can own, and how much he can control. This play is close to Strindberg's *Dream Play* in imagery. The freedom that men seek is short-lived, it is experienced for brief moments and tempts us to want to repeat the experience, but freedom is only possible in death.

Ibsen, interestingly, changes the scene only once in *The Wild Duck*. Again he is rhythmically accurate, restating the pulse and progression of the play in visual terms. One act takes place at the Werle residence, the remaining four at the Ekdal residence. Everything that was once Werle's and is now cast off ends up at the Ekdal's house to live a half-life. And to digress for a moment, Old Werle is a manufacturer and merchant, a maker and seller of things. Hialmar Ekdal is a photographer, a maker of images, which, the action of the play indicates, always need retouching.

Among the cast-offs—the by-products of the raw materials which Werle has used for his own purposes—are his son; his former mistress, Gina; his former partner, Old Ekdal; his illegitimate daughter, Hedvig; the prize of Werle's hunting expedition, the wild duck. The people, like the wild duck, live in relative comfort in spite of the fact that they have been wounded or crippled in some way—except for Gregers Werle who, dissatisfied with his lot in life, wants to become a manufacturer too. He wants to make new and better products of the cast off by-products. One of the major ironies of the play is that Gina and Hialmar are seconds. They are incapable of becoming better than they are.

There are many overlapping ironies in this play, but among them all, one idea stands out. Old Werle has touched every aspect of the Ekdal household and continues to do so. He keeps the Ekdals in a degradingly dependent position which they do not seem to mind in the least, because he keeps them physically comfortable. He is their provider. Young Werle tries to make the Ekdals dependent upon him in a spiritual sense. The Ekdals resist becoming dependent upon Gregers Werle because he would rob them of physical comfort in order to make them spiritually free.

Scenically Ibsen shows us bright, expensive, and comfortable confinement in the Werle home, where both Old and Young Ekdal feel out of place. A sense of spaciousness is suggested by the brightly lit room beyond the main room with open folding doors, and the curtains drawn back. The scene for the Ekdal's house is in one way a copy of the scene representing Werle's mansion. Repeated is the idea of a main room with a room beyond, this time marked by a double sliding door which is closed. The room is comfortable in a poorer way than Werle's, and it seems to be less "protected" and more vulnerable to nature. It is on a top floor; the panes of glass of a sloping roof open the room to the sky; in addition, the double doors enclose a garret which has been transformed into an indoor woods. Plants and animals thrive there. Have the Ekdals embraced and ordered nature? Or do those doors contain an untamed wilderness which crowds and threatens their existence? The answer is an ironic one, in that both are true. The Ekdals have fixed themselves a second-hand nature, just as they retouch photographs, and just as they retouch reality. The scene change shows us not only an ironic similarity in the room structure, which underlines the bond between the two households, but the change tells us, by its odd proportion of four acts to one, that what Werle touches for a short period of time goes on and on living in the Ekdal home either because the Ekdals allow it or actively wish it that way. Contrary to what Gregers Werle thinks, the existence in the Ekdal home is really one part Werle and four parts Ekdal. The Ekdals like things second-hand. The scene change is rhythmically accurate in that each moment that Werle is responsible for is balanced by many moments of Ekdal acceptance. Hialmar's careful tearing of the deed of gift for Hedvig is evidence enough that he hasn't the strength to fight the comforts that Old Werle provides. The arrival of Werle's gift takes a moment. The handling of it takes quite a bit of time.

Chekhov's scenic progressions are hardly linear. Neither his characters nor his dramatic action follow linear or goal-oriented patterns as Ibsen's tend to do. All Chekhov's masterpieces, similar in many ways, are also in significant ways quite different from each other. The protagonists may in each case be victimized by oblivious people who, whether selfish or well-meaning or some combination of both do irreparable harm, but the kind of harm they do varies. Since Chekhov's plays are so patterned, and since the "results" are not traceable to the machinations of one or a few characters, but rather to the pattern, the oblivious doers of harm only work as agents in pushing the protagonists closer to their particular forms of misery. The varied results might be described as follows: Treplev can only point a gun at his head a second time; Vanya and Sonya are imprisoned on the estate; the Prozorov sisters are expelled from their home and forced to separate from each other, and Lyubov and Gaev must watch their past being cut down all around them. The manners in which the protagonists reach the ends of their dramatic journeys are determined by their particular desires and the ways in which Chekhov has seen fit to frustrate them.

The visual progression for *The Cherry Orchard*, the latest and most complex of Chekhov's plays, is poetry. As Lyubov and Gaev move through the places that symbolize their past, they play out the drama of their inability to hold on to the past. Chekhov uses every symbol of beginnings in act 1: a nursery, dawn, sunrise, and May. The cherry trees are in bloom. These symbols tell us of a past which the family of Lyubov shares, but they also underline the disparity between the past and the present. The people who fill the nursery are childlike, but they are all, except Anya, long past the carefree and innocent years. Lyubov makes speeches from the nursery to the orchard, totally ignoring the repeated warnings that it is to be sold from under her. And the fate of the orchard stands for many issues in addition to Lyubov's past, among which are the love interests of Varya and Anya. Lyubov's speech to the orchard on this May morning is ironic, for the "beginnings" she talks about and the beginnings that she is in the midst of are only the beginnings of the end:

LYUBOV. . . . Oh, my childhood, my innocence! It was in this nursery I used to sleep, from here I looked out into the orchard, happiness waked with me every morning and in those days the orchard was just the same, nothing has changed (*laughs with delight*). All, all white! Oh, my orchard! After the dark gloomy autumn, and the cold winter; you are young again, and full of happiness, the heavenly angels have never left you. . . . If I could cast off the burden that weighs on my heart, if I could forget the past!   (Pp. 75–76)

Act 2 shows the fate of the orchard being sealed. It does not really happen in act 3, as Lyubov pretends to herself. And we know something of that fate by the scene change. The scene provides symbols of the fading of ripeness—midsummer, afternoon. The sun sets during the act. And the most striking visual image is that of the characters sitting between the orchard and the old tombstones. The orchard, first seen from a nursery (by both Lyubov and an audience) is now seen from a shrine. As the characters sit mid-day, mid-season, mid-life and death, the orchard is lost. It is in this act that Lyubov lunches in town, calls Lopahin's plan for villas vulgar, and gives the last of her money to a wayfarer. Gaev, too, shows that the orchard is hopelessly lost: "GAEV *(puts a caramel in his mouth)*. 'They say I've eaten up my property in caramels' *(laughs)*" (p. 86).

In act 3 the orchard is totally out of sight, only to be more in mind. It is lost; the fact needs only to be stated verbally. It is stated visually in that a party of people dance to a Jewish orchestra which Lyubov cannot afford in a room from which the orchard cannot be seen. Merrymaking goes on, contrapuntal to Lyubov's doom, and *"it is evening"* (p. 94).

The scene for act 4 comments not only on the fact that the past is gone, but that new beginnings are bleak. The new life is thin and poor compared to the richness of the old life. How better to show us the end of the progression than to put us back into the nursery, which is bare.

> *Same as in First Act. There are neither curtains on the windows nor pictures on the walls: only a little furniture remains piled up in a corner as if for sale. There is a sense of desolation; near the outer door and in the background of the scene are packed trunks, travelling bags, etc.* (P. 107)

Since Chekhov indicates there are no curtains on the windows, we may assume we see the bare trees of October as we hear the strokes of the ax cutting their fellows down in another part of the orchard.

Chekhov associates many issues with the cherry orchard and its fate, and he shows us the fate of all the play's sympathetic issues through his visual progression. The major progression is a combination of linear, circular, and indirectly balanced patterns or minor progressions. The combination is part of the reason a Chekhovian pattern is so complex and part of the reason why we cannot label it so easily. That is why, too, we talk about the plural rhythms of Chekhov. The progression of places in which the action takes place and from which the orchard is viewed (or not viewed) is one of indirect balance—from the nursery, from the tomb, not at all, from the nursery. The progression from May to October is more linear, and reminds us that no matter how everything else is balanced, time goes on. The progression from sunrise to sunset to evening to sometime midday is almost circular but the circle has already begun to repeat itself: it is past morning in the new life.

Several progressions are combined as well in *The Three Sisters*, and the sisters are expelled from their family home, although in not quite the same way Lyubov was from hers. The Prozorov sisters would like to leave their home willingly to go to Moscow, but instead they must simply leave it to go to places much less exciting and much closer to home. In this play, Chekhov writes an interrupted progression in terms of seasonal change: from spring to winter to some undefined season to fall; a circular progression in terms of the time of day: midday to evening to the middle of the night to noon; and an extremely interesting double direction in terms of space. There is indirect balance in this last progression. The sisters dream their dreams of Moscow in a spacious drawing room of which they are in control in act 1, a drawing room cramped by Natasha's rules in act 2, a crowded bedroom where the sisters have been driven together in act 3, and finally the outdoors. The scenic progression, then, is from increasing confinement to expulsion. First the sisters are pushed into a corner and then not even afforded the protection of that corner. Robert Brustein calls this a playing out of dispossession, and he relates it to the dispossession of Lyubov. He points out that the sisters are gradually pushed outside, and he points out seasonal progression in *The Cherry Orchard*; but he is not concerned with relating all of the progressions as progressions.[1]

Chekhov's scene changes tend to be ironic in that they both support the action and comment upon it. Chekhov has a dreadful habit of showing the passage of time through days and seasons while the change of place only spells increasing disaster to the protagonists. He has a dreadful habit too of giving the protagonists half of what they want—the wrong half—almost as if a prayer were heard and misunderstood. Lyubov cries: "If I could forget the past!" (act 1, p. 76), and the richest part of her past is pulled from under her. Irina phrases the yearning of all three sisters "to go back to Moscow. To sell the house, to make an end of everything here, and off to Moscow . . ." (act 1, p. 122). And they eventually leave the house behind them, only to live apart from each other and far from Moscow. Vanya fights hard for the estate: "The estate is free from debt and in a good condition only owing to my personal efforts. And now that I am old I am to be kicked out of it!" (act 3, p. 229) only to be kicked back onto it without faith in the professor or the presence of Yelena to brighten his existence. Treplev and Nina want to become artists so that they can express themselves. They do become artists, but nobody understands them. Treplev's readers think he is an old man; Nina's few successful moments have been when she cried well, or died well.

The scenic progression of *Uncle Vanya* supports Vanya's having been kicked back onto the estate. The scene changes give an image of increasing imprisonment, but the attendant changes of day and season provide progressive images of ripeness to harvest. Chekhov moves the characters from outdoors to indoors to Vanya's room where there is *"a cage with a starling in it"* (p. 234). The first two acts take place in summer, the second two in autumn. In the first act it is a cloudy midafternoon, in the second a rainy midnight. In the third it is early afternoon, in the fourth evening. Not only does the action of the play span summer and early fall, but "late" moments of the day in summer, and earlier moments of the day in fall. This is a play grounded in the despair of the middle years of existence. *Uncle Vanya* is a play without youthful spirit. It possesses no dreaming Irina or Anya. Sonya may not be very old in years, but in spirit, she is fast approaching middle age. She has not been blessed with beauty, and beauty might have been her fountain of youth. There are no young characters for balance, and all the major characters are caught in the moment of passing "ripeness" or hope in their lives. Vanya and Astrov are concerned with how they have wasted their years, and how the years have wasted them. Yelena's beauty represents to both of them a potential spark of youth. Sonya and Yelena watch their own youths disappearing without love, and Astrov's magnetism represents excitement which might give them new energy. The scenic changes rhythmically beat out the meanings of the play. As Vanya and Sonya are pushed into the workroom, the double images of day to night (from 1 to 2, and from 3 to 4), the overall image of summer to fall reminds us that time will not wait for Vanya and Sonya. They have approached the evening and autumn of their lives without fulfillment.

In the earliest of Chekhov's masterpieces, *The Sea Gull*, scenic rhythm is not so "perfect" as in the other plays, but it is nevertheless an accurate underlining of the play's values. The patterns that Chekhov developed appear here in more primitive form. The times of day are indicated as evening, midday, midday, evening. There is a general movement from outdoors (acts 1 and 2) to indoors (acts 3 and 4). And there is a complex progression scenically from relative disorder to order in the first half of the play, and from relative order to disorder in the second half. Act 1 is Treplev's act; he is in possession of our attentions and is the focal point of the action. The scene gives us an appropriate image. The stage that Treplev has built is an intrusion on the landscape, for it blocks the lake. Yet ironically he means to use the lake, to use nature raw, for his play. The result of his play is, of course, that his meanings are obscure to his audience.

The croquet lawn of act 2 finds Arkadina in possession; it is a more ordered image of nature as Arkadina's life is more ordered than either Treplev's or Nina's. And if the scene for act 3, the dining room containing luggage and evidences of planned departure, is not exactly orderly, it is still more ordered than Treplev's quarters of act 4. The drawing room is still a drawing room, but a corner of it comprises a study for Treplev, while during the act it is put to a third use—a bedroom for Sorin who is dying. The outdoors is partially visible and Medvedenko describes in detail what we cannot see fully so that our imaginations are at work conjuring up an image of the place from which Nina will appear. Early in the act, Medvedenko says: "How dark it is in the garden! We ought to have told them to break up that stage in the garden. It stands as bare and ugly as a skeleton, and the curtain flaps in the wind. When I passed it yesterday evening, it seemed as though someone were crying in it" (p. 43). It is important that act 4 is Treplev's act, just as acts 2 and 3, with their more ordered scenes, belonged primarily to Arkadina and Trigorin, the more "orderly" and conventional artists. Act 4 is the end of the beginning Treplev made in act 1. His readers think of him as an old man. Sorin is his companion. And the summer of the first three acts is resolved in the autumn of the fourth, two years later.

Chekhov's mastery of rhythmic scene change is reflected in the number of rhythms he combines in the overall pattern of changes—including dialogue rhythms, character rhythms, and so forth. The fact that he shows such complexity in scene change alone hints at the staggering number of overlapping rhythms that fill each play. And yet in each case, all work together in intricate relationships toward "the final aim of the artist."

Rhythm of scene change seems especially poetic in the masterpieces of realistic tragedy and dark comedy. A related, but different use of rhythmic scene change operates in Shaw's *Arms and the Man*. He does not "poeticize" the play with his scene changes; he is not particularly concerned with seasonal change or times of day or images of light and freedom. But then this is not tragedy, and it is brighter comedy than Chekhov's. The inhabitants of the Petkoff household are healthy and robust seekers of life. It so happens that their pretensions to grandeur and nobility repeatedly get in their way. That is the joke of Shaw's play. And that is the repeated joke in his scene changes. The play deals with the romantic ideals about love and war which are contradicted by the facts of love and war; the human capacity for fantasy is mocked by practical reality. Yet practical reality is often shown to be a reversal of or an upside-down image of a romantic ideal, in its way just as "romantic" as its opposite extreme. Bluntschli carries chocolates into battle instead of cartridges. He has found them more useful. But is this really practical or just another romantic image, an upside-down version of the seasoned soldier of fortune? Repeated in the scene changes is the irony of the combination of the real and the ideal, the practial and the romantic. Act 1 is set in Raina Petkoff's bedroom (which was meant to have a certain amount of shock value to its 1894 audience). Shaw describes the bedroom as unlike anything known to the other "side" of Europe. *"It is half rich Bulgarian, half cheap Viennese."* For instance, *"the counterpane and hangings of the bed, the window curtains, the little carpet, and all the ornamental textile fabrics in the room are oriental and gorgeous; the paper on the walls is occidental and paltry."*[2] Viennese touches in Raina's room as well as in her character are "imported." They are her attempts to be better than Bulgarian. She tells Bluntschli, who is falling asleep on his feet, that the Petkoffs possess a library:

RAINA *(affectedly)*. I tell you these things to shew you that you are not in the house of ignorant country folk who would kill you the moment they saw your Serbian uniform, but among civilized people. We go to Bucharest every year for the opera season; and I have spent a whole month in Vienna. (P. 405).

The attempt of the Petkoffs to civilize themselves and their house is reflected again in act 2. Shaw sets the act in the Petkoffs' garden, from which the gorgeous Balkan landscape can be seen. However, the fruit bushes around the house are *"covered with washing spread out to dry"* (p. 408). Even such a simple scene as this gives rise to a discussion about what is correct and civilized in the world beyond Bulgaria. Petkoff has just warned his wife against washing her neck every day, which he considers a ridiculously impractical civility.

PETKOFF. I dont mind a good wash once a week to keep up my position; but once a day is carrying the thing to a ridiculous extreme.

CATHERINE. You are a barbarian at heart still, Paul. I hope you behaved yourself before all those Russian officers.

PETKOFF. I did my best. I took care to let them know that we have a library.

CATHERINE. Ah; but you didnt tell them that we have an electric bell in it? I have had one put up.

PETKOFF. Whats an electric bell?

CATHERINE. You touch a button; something tinkles in the kitchen; and then Nicola comes up.

PETKOFF. Why not shout for him?

CATHERINE. Civilized people never shout for their servants. Ive learnt that while you were away.

PETKOFF. Well, Ill tell you something Ive learnt too. Civilized people dont hang out their washing to dry where visitors can see it: so youd better have all that *(indicating the clothes on the bushes)* put somewhere else.

CATHERINE. Oh, thats absurd, Paul: I dont believe really refined people notice such things.   (Pp. 411–12)

Act 3 finally shows us the library which has figured so prominently in all discussions of the refined and civilized life which no one in Bulgaria except the Petkoffs has realized so well. It is Shaw's final scenic joke. He has been building to it all along. The library, of course, is a comic library, almost devoid of books. Moreover, it, too, has a few of the persistent homespun elements which the Petkoffs cannot seem to rid themselves of. Here are the highlights of Shaw's description:

> In the library after lunch. It is not much of a library. Its literary equipment consists of a single fixed shelf stocked with old paper covered novels, broken backed, coffee stained, torn and thumbed; and a couple of little hanging shelves with a few gift books on them:

the rest of the wall space being occupied by trophies of war and the chase. But it is a most comfortable sitting room. . . . There is one object, however, hopelessly out of keeping with its surroundings. This is a small kitchen table, much the worse for wear, fitted as a writing table with an old canister full of pens, an eggcup filled with ink, and a deplorable scrap of heavily used pink blotting paper.

(P. 426)

And so with the kitchen table, the eggcup, and so forth, practicality invades the Petkoff household again in spite of its pretensions to grandeur. Shaw's progression is unified. There is something of "home" in each scene to "tattle" on the Petkoffs. And the alternations of cold and refined things with warm and homespun elements is itself rhythmic since we look at each scene in logical groupings. However, a great deal of Shaw's effect (and his intent, no doubt) results from a combined verbal and visual joke. We finally get to see the library which we have heard about for two acts. And it is a perfect final statement on the family.

The rhythm of a limited scenic progression is an important one in the plays which utilize it. It makes us aware of progression in the action and it does so by reminding us of what is stable or repeated throughout, what changes, and what the stops along the way in the progression are. It is a kind of rhythm very appropriate to realistic and naturalistic plays because it makes progression seem logical, and because it provides a visual clue to the changes that are occurring in a more abstract sense. Rhythmically the limited progression emphasizes the unity of change. It strikes some middle ground between the single scene in which once stability is emphasized we watch for the minor change, and the panoramic approach in which so much changes that we watch for the sameness or stability in the progression.

Symbolic Gesture

In most cases it has been impossible to discuss the rhythm of the scene without referring to the relationship of scenic rhythm to the overall action of the play, to the rhythm of lighting when appropriate, and in some cases to specific lines of dialogue. This is as it should be, since all rhythms of a play are very much related to each other. Costume changes (or the absence of change), as well as properties which are visual symbols, operate rhythmically in drama, much the same as the overall scene does. Indeed these visual elements are part of the visual rhythm. And the same principles that govern other rhythms—repetition, change, and progression—govern their use as well. The black dresses of Chekhov's Mashas make repeated statements and remain stable through changes that happen to their wearers. The garb of Shaw's Catherine Petkoff restates the joke of the play. She is described as follows for her first appearance in the comedy: *"a woman over forty, imperiously energetic, with magnificent black hair and eyes, who might be a very splendid specimen of the wife of a mountain farmer, but is determined to be a Viennese lady, and to that end wears a fashionable tea gown on all occasions."*[1] Act 2 confirms her combined practicality and pretensions to grandeur: *"Catherine, who, having at this early hour made only a very perfunctory toilet, wears a Bulgarian apron over a once brilliant but now half worn-out dressing gown, and a colored handkerchief tied over her thick*

157

black hair, comes from the house with Turkish slippers on her bare feet, looking astonishingly handsome and stately under all the circumstances" (p. 410). Shaw gets a comic moment later in act 2 when Catherine throws the apron and the handkerchief behind a bush to make herself presentable to Bluntschli.

The use of properties as visual symbols may be rhythmic, as well; for instance, Hedda's pistols in *Hedda Gabler* provide an important progression. Hedda first uses them verbally to wound Tesman because he cannot afford a man in livery or a saddle horse. The reference, which ends act 1, is important climactically. As a result, the issue is planted in our minds:

HEDDA. . . . Well, I shall have one thing at least to kill time with in the meanwhile.

TESMAN *(beaming)*. Oh, thank heaven for that! What is it, Hedda? Eh?

HEDDA *(in the middle doorway, looks at him with covert scorn)*. My pistols, George.

TESMAN *(in alarm)*. Your pistols!

HEDDA *(with cold eyes)*. General Gabler's pistols.

   (She goes out through the inner room, to the left.)

TESMAN *(rushes up to the middle doorway and calls after her)*. No, for heaven's sake, Hedda darling—don't touch those dangerous things! For my sake, Hedda! Eh? (Pp. 175–76)

In the beginning of act 2, Hedda points a pistol at Judge Brack for "sneaking in by the back way" (p. 176). One of the pair of pistols is given to Lövborg in act 3 because Hedda, knowing she can give him nothing else, gives him the means of self-destruction. And finally, after her war with all the men in the play, when the judge blackmails her with his knowledge that it is one of her pistols in the hands of the police, Hedda must turn the remaining pistol to her own temple. The use of the prop or visual symbol is rhythmically sound; there is the repetition of an element, with changes, pointing to a progression. Repeated use of the pistol points up the variations or changes in its use. It is appropriate that the symbol should be used to worry Tesman, to play a dangerous game with Brack, to destroy Lövborg "secretly," only to result in a number of reversals in act 4. Hedda finds that she had no hand in Lövborg's destiny, nor was his death "beautiful." Brack is playing a dangerous game with Hedda in which the pistol is his weapon. And Tesman continues to underestimate her. Even when Hedda kills herself, Tesman's first reaction is worry that "she is playing with those pistols again" (p. 221).

Hedda's pistols are certainly symbolic, but they are ironically symbolic as all of Ibsen's symbols are. Caroline W. Mayerson writes of the pistols as well as other symbolic elements in an essay entitled "Thematic Symbols in *Hedda Gabler*." But she deals with the pistols as psychological symbols of what is wrong with Hedda rather than dramatic symbols indicating what is right with Ibsen. Mayerson says she is concerned with the ironic plot function of the pistols, and she explains accurately the melodramatic flourishes with which Hedda points the gun at Brack in act 2 and with which she obviously pointed it at Lövborg sometime in the past to "warn encroachments on her 'honor.'" However, she finds irony in the "clouded perspective" of Hedda's view of and use of the pistols. And she feels that the irony of the end of the play is based on Hedda's "inability to perceive the difference between melodrama and tragedy," since she takes her own death as a serious and significant statement.[2] The play can certainly be played that way, with Hedda confused, full of self-delusions, gun at temple. However, the lines that she speaks and the rhythm of the use of the pistols support the interpretation of her acts as conscious ones, informed by intelligence. States explains the Ibsen protagonist's habit of "overseeing." The Ibsen character is perfectly aware of symbols as symbols and has an important hand in manipulating them.[3] Hedda, in fact, seems totally aware of when she is playing with the pistols melodramatically and when she is playing with them destructively. And, in fact, she arranges her suicide so well, so artistically, that it is difficult to imagine she is not *still* trying to achieve some effect on those who have left her behind. She seems to be saying with her suicide, "I will confound them all!" At any rate, there is a perfectly patterned and rhythmic use of the pistols: they are used more and more dangerously from acts 1 to 3; they are turned against Hedda by the victims in act 4, and as Hedda understands, she must have a hand in turning them against herself. She must at least be able to control her own destiny.

Visual rhythms, then, may include the clothes of the characters and the things of the characters as well as the places, seasons, and times of the action. One other very important visual rhythm is difficult to ignore, and it is also so pervasive that it is difficult to isolate. It does not fit so easily into the categories of person, place, or thing. And that is the overall rhythm of a play's mimetic action: what is imitated or played out in the *physical sense*. This area may seem to have much more to do with the director's and actor's functions than it does with the playwright's creation. And indeed a director or actor may interpret accurately and heighten the effects or he may misinterpret and do damage to the playwright's intent—just as the scene designer, costume designer, or lighting designer may throw off the rhythm of a play by not paying careful attention to what is written and what is meant by the written word. All too often lines are cut or entrances are changed or business is invented which throw off the rhythm of the scene or of the whole play. In one production Tartuffe entered several times in act 1, ruining the rhythmic buildup to his entrance in act 2. Less extreme examples of "not understanding the parts" of a play may be found in productions in which exits are made lines earlier or later than the playwright intended, thereby spoiling an important "effect." A more extreme example is a production of *Waiting for Godot* minus Pozzo and Lucky. We might well wonder to what extent those interruptions and returns to sameness made sense without the "big interruptions."

If we imagine some of the plays discussed above with the sound turned off so that we see only the visual changes, we may perhaps be more aware of the repetitions, changes, and progressions that the playwrights have "written in" as part of the

visual drama in addition to the scenic change and its close relations. Those changes are based on the dialogue, and some of
them have been referred to in discussions of attitude rhythm
and scenic rhythm. They are the changes in the visual drama
that are effected by (1) how many characters are on stage, (2)
who they are to each other, and (3) what happens between
them. In other words they are the answers to the question, Who
does what to whom and in what context? It is an extremely big
issue and seems to encompass all of drama itself; but with a
simpler perspective, it is at the heart of what might be called
the rhythm of symbolic gesture. Included is the repeated metaphoric gesture of *Waiting for Godot:* Vladimir pulls Estragon up.
Estragon draws Vladimir down. It is an action that happens
often enough and with enough variety to be a rhythmic progression. Included is the progression in *The Sea Gull* that makes visible the separation of Treplev and Nina. They are together in act
1, together for a brief moment in act 2 (the handing over of the
sea gull), never seen together in act 3, and together again, needless to say with ironic results, in act 4. Included too is the incredibly brief arrival in, and departure from, the garden of
Serebryakov and Yelena in act 1 of *Uncle Vanya* and their very
brief arrival in, and departure from, Vanya's room in act 4,
reflecting the major event of the play: their arrival at, and departure from, the estate and from Vanya's life. The rhythm of
pantomime or metaphoric gesture is dependent upon the characters' function as symbols. Their presence or absence from
the stage and their repeated gestures are elements of a visual
rhythm.

No matter how structurally similar (and therefore rhythmically similar) certain plays of a particular style and period
seem, differences in patterning are important and point to the
meaning of each work. Sophocles' *Oedipus* and Euripides' *Hippolytus* are patterned differently in terms of symbolic gesture.
Oedipus has interviews with several other characters in investigating the murder of Laius. He is the constant in the scene.
The other characters come and go, but he remains confronting

each of them. Because no important furthering of the action goes on without Oedipus until the resolution when he blinds himself offstage, Sophocles achieves a strong and regular pulse to the play as well as the focused action we are so well aware of. Each confrontation between Oedipus and some other character reflects the direct ill will of Apollo for Oedipus. Each character seems to bring some freedom for Oedipus; each character, relatively innocent, is subject to Oedipus' wrath. The gesture of interrogation is repeated by Oedipus throughout.

The direct battle in *Oedipus* is perhaps clearer by comparison with the more indirect battle of *Hippolytus*. In Euripides' play, Aphrodite does not battle Hippolytus directly, but includes Phaedra and Theseus in her scheme, because they are convenient. Once the machinery is set in motion, Phaedra and Hippolytus do not confront each other directly either, but Phaedra's love-agony is related to Hippolytus by the nurse, and Hippolytus' rage is directed to the air and to the nurse, but not to Phaedra. No one character remains through all scenes. In fact, Theseus almost replaces Phaedra (the same actor played both) as the human agent carrying out Hippolytus' destruction. A false tablet speaks for Phaedra to Theseus, just as the nurse was Phaedra's false messenger to Hippolytus. Nor, because of the oath that he swore, can Hippolytus engage in a truthful and direct confrontation with Theseus. Even Artemis' promised revenge on Aphrodite is indirect and can ironically do nothing to help Phaedra, Hippolytus, or Theseus. Artemis' words of cold comfort are: "For upon one, her minion, with mine hand— / One who is dearest of all men to her— / With these unerring shafts will I avenge me."[4]

In Euripides' play what we do not see (as opposed to what we see, hear, and know to be true) is as repetitive an element as is necessary to sense a rhythmic rightness. We see substitutions for confrontations. We do not see Aphrodite confront Hippolytus, Phaedra confront Hippolytus, Hippolytus confront Phaedra, or Artemis confront Aphrodite. We do see Theseus con-

front his son, but that too is a substitution, for his wrath should
be directed at the nurse, Phaedra, and ultimately at the gods,
but he does not know it. A sense of mystery and deviousness is
achieved partly by changing the focal characters constantly,
leaving no one hero to stay on stage the whole time and deal
with all tragic consequences.

Shakespeare's *Hamlet* and *Antony and Cleopatra* each show
us a different series of pictures of character clustering and the
rhythm of the action. Shakespeare presents Hamlet alone a
good many times. And when he is not alone in a physical sense,
he is usually alone in spirit. He is not a comfortable part of Claudius' court, nor one with his fellows after he has seen the ghost.
He resists Rosencrantz and Guildenstern and generally sends
Polonius into tailspins. He is alone even when he is not alone; he
is on the outside of the action. Claudius, on the other hand, is always surrounded by counsellors, protectors, followers, ambas-
sadors, or the like until the prayer scene, when he becomes a
vulnerable and sympathetic villain. We are rhythmically prepared for this soliloquy by all Claudius' public scenes and by all
Hamlet's soliloquies prior to this scene. And we are forced to
see some similarity between the antagonists—if in nothing else
than in introspective soul-searching. The recurring visual images of Hamlet either alone or isolated in a group are part of the
rhythm of the play. Another element of the visual rhythm, repeated by analogy and repeated by several characters, is the
action of investigation.[5] Sleuthing is the mode, the "how" and
therefore the rhythm of the action, Boleslavsky would insist. Investigation is a recurring element, sometimes handled verbally
(Polonius is investigating through Reynaldo the doings of Laertes), but often shown visually. Hamlet's play within the play is a
detective's trap; Polonius and Claudius hide behind an arras to
observe Hamlet; Polonius hides behind an arras once too often
in Gertrude's chambers; Hamlet and Horatio withdraw to
watch the funeral procession. These are the broadest examples, but as a rhythmic device, these physicalized investigations

point the way to Hamlet's and the play's most important investigations—those of a philosophical nature concerning life and death, guilt and punishment.

Antony and Cleopatra has few scenes of solitariness, and its repeated gestures are not those of investigation. The first element of visual rhythm that comes to our attention, though, is the sheer numbers of characters who fill the stage. Those people we are to think of as powerful are always surrounded by a host of followers and servants. Antony, Cleopatra, Caesar, and Pompey are lent stature, and the play is lent grandeur, by the many minor dramatis personae. Even when Antony's men have supposedly left him, he still retains enough of them on stage to look like a leader of men and to keep this play in the realm of "bright" tragedy.

One could go on at length about the reversals in the play—the politics in love and the emotions of war, the vacillating of whole crowds and the vacillating of the principal characters, particularly Antony who cannot stay with Cleopatra and cannot leave her. But as discussed before, this quality of constant reversal—"The present pleasure, / By revolution lowering does become / The opposite of itself" (1.2.128–30)—is constantly reinforced by what we see and experience through the alternation of emotional scenes with scenes of restraint. The complex combination of these "types" was discussed earlier with regard to scene change. And the sense of scope is supported by having masses of followers of the principals marching across the stage, telling us that the characters are big and the stakes are big.

There is a rhythm of gesture, however, which helps to ground the action and which informs us quite early that the play must end in Egypt and must end with Cleopatra. The first element of this picturization is Cleopatra's seeming passivity. It is ingenious of Shakespeare to have created so volatile a character as Cleopatra, to have made her an aggressive lover and a willing warrior, and to have given us the impression at the same time that she "stays put." He seems to have accomplished this in two ways. First, Cleopatra is the only power who stays at home.

Pompey is roaming the seas, Caesar marches on other countries, Antony travels from Egypt to Rome, even Octavia is "on the road." Cleopatra's identity with Egypt becomes strong by comparison with the travelers in this play. And second, time seems to move more slowly in Egypt, because of the double time scheme. A great deal happens in Rome between the two scenes in which Cleopatra deals with the unfortunate messenger who brings news of Antony's marriage. Egypt and Cleopatra become the stiller accents to the movement in this play.

Shakespeare uses another device too. When Cleopatra does move, she is likely to move away from trouble, to leave conflict, and her leaving creates a vacuum, making others follow her. The most famous example, of course, is the verbal relation of the battle scene, when her ships left the fray, only to be followed by Antony's ships. But there is plenty of rhythmic preparation for this important moment. It is, in fact, Cleopatra's way. She leaves and pretends to leave everything that hints at potential trouble. In act 1, scene 2, Cleopatra calls Antony to her, but the very moment he arrives, she says, "We will not look upon him. Go with us" (1.2.91). And her followers follow her out. She threatens to leave as soon as Antony enters in the next scene with a melodramatic performance of agony: "Help me away, dear Charmian, I shall fall, / It cannot be thus long, the sides of nature / Will not sustain it" (1.3.15–17). Her later retreat to the monument accomplishes the same end. Antony, thinking she is dead, immediately sets out to follow her.

The gesture of "leaving" or retreating is not confined to Cleopatra alone, although she is certainly well seasoned in the art. The play follows the other leavers as Antony follows Cleopatra. Caesar's first concern with Antony is that he has abandoned his calling as a warrior and statesman, and he is not content until he gets Antony back to Rome. When Antony leaves Rome, and when he eventually leaves Octavia, the characters and the play follow him. Enobarbus, by his leaving, betrays Antony. And leaving has meant betrayal before in this play. It operates as a device meaning both betrayal and the drawing force of the magnetic characters in the play. The more they retreat to privacy, the more armies come rushing after them.

Every good play has a visual rhythm of character placement, pantomime, and gesture. Interrogation, investigation, and retreat, for example, may appear in many forms and with a great deal of variety, but their repetition as actions with variety is rhythmic. The rhythm of gesture is so much a part of the total action that were a play to be staged "with the sound turned off" a good deal of the meaning would remain intact. The subtleties of verbal irony and imagery would be lost of course, and I am not suggesting such a treatment of dramatic works, but the fact remains that the playwrights we love and admire most write for the eyes as well as the ears. And that being the case, visual elements must have rhythm. The visual elements of a play do have rhythm—repetition, change, and progression—in the setting, visual symbols, and character placement (entrances and exits included) because the characters are, after all, visual symbols too.

The Interrelationship of Rhythms

So far it has been clear that any one pattern in progression in a play is a reflection of other like patterns, that rhythm is a unifying device. Moreover, the better the play, the more complex its rhythmic patterns are likely to be. I said earlier that great plays, like *Hamlet, Uncle Vanya,* and *Waiting for Godot,* are filled with examples of every sort of dialogue rhythm. It is also true that these plays have illustrated to us some of the most complex uses of visual rhythms as well. In great plays, where rhythms are juggled constantly and more than one rhythm appears simultaneously, the questions arise, How do these rhythms operate together to unify rather than dissipate our impressions? Can every rhythm be of equal importance or are some of those rhythmic patterns "just there"—not to be taken notice of? In isolating particular types of rhythm, I meant to imply that the type discussed was the primary or unifying rhythm for that particular passage in my reading of the play. Since complex plays have many rhythms operating at the same time, those plays are capable of more than one interpretation. *Hamlet,* for instance, can be and has been a play about political intrigue, about sexual frustration, about a particular kind of psychological character, about disenchanted youth and the establishment, and about Renaissance life and its attendant religious and moral questions. It has also been about all of the above and more when a reader, critic, or producer has unified all of the play's

167

issues under a more philosophical umbrella pointing out ironies about love, knowledge, aggression, guilt and punishment, and life and death. All great plays carry with them the danger of reduction. There is so much there that one can either deal with it all or pick and choose according to one's fancy. It seems to me better to deal with multiple rhythms when they exist, to attempt to understand how they fit together, to grant the play in question its due complexity. The following is an attempt to point out the many patterns operating in a key scene in *Hamlet* and to study the interrelationships of those patterns in motion.

In act 4, scene 4, of *Hamlet*—the "for an eggshell" scene—a number of rhythmic patterns is in operation. Stylistically, the scene is very much a part of the rest of the play and echoes many of its established features: the scene is composed primarily of blank verse, language that is vital and exciting and inventive; the setting does not need to be realized in very specific terms, therefore the platform that holds the action, and the entrances and exits from that platform, take on a highly symbolic quality; the characters, too, are part of a symbolic arrangement in that a limited number of actors is used to represent an army. In other words, the characteristics of Renaissance drama and of Shakespearean drama, both, are part of the voice that ties this scene to the rest of the play. Within the overall rhythm of style are other rhythms. The rhythm of speaker alternation is a major one—one of the larger threads of patterning in this scene. Again, as in several other scenes of this play, relatively brief speeches give way to lengthy expression, in this case, another soliloquy in excess of thirty lines from Hamlet.

The scene follows. Both in overall style and in the pattern of speaker alternation it is inextricably tied to the rest of the play.

(Enter FORTINBRAS *with his* ARMY *led by* CAPTAIN.*)*
FORTINBRAS. Go captain, from me greet the Danish King;
   Tell him, that by his licence Fortinbras
   Craves the conveyance of a promised march
   Over his kingdom. You know the rendezvous.
   If that his Majesty would aught with us,

We shall express our duty in his eye,
And let him know so.

CAPTAIN.   I will do't my lord.

FORTINBRAS. Go softly on.

(Exeunt all but CAPTAIN.)

(Enter HAMLET, ROSENCRANTZ, GUILDENSTERN, and others.)

HAMLET. Good sir, whose powers are these?

CAPTAIN. They are of Norway sir.

HAMLET. How purposed sir I pray you?

CAPTAIN. Against some part of Poland.

HAMLET. Who commands them sir?

CAPTAIN. The nephew to old Norway, Fortinbras.

HAMLET. Goes it against the main of Poland sir,
Or for some frontier?

CAPTAIN. Truly to speak, and with no addition,
We go to gain a little patch of ground
That hath in it no profit but the name.
To pay five ducats, five, I would not farm it;
Nor will it yield to Norway or the Pole
A ranker rate, should it be sold in fee.

HAMLET. Why then the Polack never will defend it.

CAPTAIN. Yes, it is already garrisoned.

HAMLET. Two thousand souls, and twenty thousand ducats,
Will not debate the question of this straw.
This is th' imposthume of much wealth and peace,
That inward breaks, and shows no cause without
Why the man dies. I humbly thank you sir.

CAPTAIN. God buy you sir.   *(Exit.)*

ROSENCRANTZ.   Will't please you go my lord?

HAMLET. I'll be with you straight, go a little before.

(Exeunt all but HAMLET.)

How all occasions do inform against me,
And spur my dull revenge! What is a man,
If his chief good and market of his time
Be but to sleep and feed? A beast, no more.
Sure he that made us with such large discourse,
Looking before and after, gave us not
That capability and godlike reason
To fust in us unused. Now whether it be
Bestial oblivion, or some craven scruple

Of thinking too precisely on th' event—
A thought which quartered hath but one part wisdom,
And ever three parts coward—I do not know
Why yet I live to say, this thing's to do,
Sith I have cause, and will, and strength, and means
To do't. Examples gross as earth exhort me.
Witness this army of such mass and charge,
Led by a delicate and tender Prince;
Whose spirit with divine ambition puffed
Makes mouths at the invisible event,
Exposing what is mortal, and unsure,
To all that fortune, death, and danger dare,
Even for an eggshell. Rightly to be great,
Is not to stir without great argument,
But greatly to find quarrel in a straw
When honour's at the stake. How stand I then
That have a father killed, a mother stained,
Excitements of my reason, and my blood,
And let all sleep, while to my shame I see
The imminent death of twenty thousand men,
That for a fantasy and trick of fame
Go to their graves like beds; fight for a plot
Whereon the numbers cannot try the cause,
Which is not tomb enough and continent
To hide the slain? O from this time forth,
My thoughts be bloody, or be nothing worth.   *(Exit.)*

The scene would not be particularly exciting, however, if it
accomplished nothing more than echoing a number of other
scenes in the play. This scene is particularly interesting because of the rhythm of attitude change or the structuring of
character relationships. Fortinbras, with great brevity and formality, orders the Captain to convey a firm, friendly, and altogether political message to Claudius. The Captain does not hesi-
tate. The exchange is brief. And it is composed of nothing but
statements—no questions, exclamations or emotional givings
out of any sort. Hamlet enters and his exchange with the Captain is markedly different. The Captain is for all intents and

purposes an equal to Hamlet. Hamlet draws him out, listens to his opinion on the war. The exchange is patterned in questions and answers, with Hamlet, as usual, the questioner. The whole feel of the stage changes. Fortinbras made us expect physical action. Hamlet stops the play again, delighting us in mental action. The third major attitude change of the scene occurs in the soliloquy where exclamation, or the letting out of emotions amid analysis, is the key tone. Moreover, if we divide the scene mathematically, an interesting pattern emerges to view. The scene seems to "grow" in the size of its units. Fortinbras's exchange comprises eight lines, Hamlet's questions comprise eight, the more equal trading of ideas between Hamlet and the Captain, nearly sixteen lines, and Hamlet's soliloquy, thirty-four. The scene not only moves from order and constraint (Fortinbras) to lack of order (Hamlet is left alone) and expression (Hamlet is left alone for another soliloquy), but it grows in close to mathematically perfect units. Hamlet's soliloquy is longer than the "perfect" thirty-two lines, but that may account somewhat for the perfectly appropriate feeling that his last thought, "O, from this time forth, / My thoughts be bloody, or be nothing worth!" is, in the deepest sense, "tacked on," for Hamlet is forcing himself to think like the rest of the world. In other words, to quit thinking.

Speaker patterning provides the bigger rhythmic sweep; attitude patterning organizes the changes within speaker patterning. The verbal strategy of this scene, a subtler form of rhythm, is "pronounced" twice. The strategy of insistent inclusion is significant in this key scene. Just as Hamlet delays the killing of Claudius by gathering information through the whole play, he delays his embarkation to England by gathering information in this scene. He stops on what is presumably the way to a waiting ship to talk to the Captain. His questions not only accomplish a holding action in this scene, but remind us of the many other times that strategy has been employed and prepare us, too, for its future employment. The strategy is a link. We have heard the insistence upon facts, causes, and reasons in Hamlet's early scene with Rosencrantz and Guildenstern, for example. Here are some of Hamlet's questions. They smack of more than idle curiosity. This information, too, can be applied, Hamlet seems to be saying.

> What players are they?
> How chances it they travel? Their residence, both in reputation and profit, was better both ways.
> Do they hold the same estimation they did when I was in the city? Are they so followed?
> How comes it? Do they grow rusty?
> What, are they children? Who maintains 'em? How are they escoted? Will they pursue the quality no longer than they can sing? Will they not say afterwards, if they should grow themselves to common players—as it is most like, if their means are no better, their writers do them wrong to make them exclaim against their own succession?
> Is't possible?
> Do the boys carry it away? (2.2)

We will hear that insistence again the next time Hamlet appears, in the graveyard scene.

> How long hast thou been grave-maker?
> How long is that since?
> Ay marry, why was he sent into England?
> Why?
> How came he mad?
> How strangely?
> Upon what ground?
> How long will a man lie i' th' earth ere he rot?
> Why he more than another? (5.1)

In each case, the half-childlike curiosity, half-legalistic thoroughness resolves itself in a philosophical comparison: Hamlet compares the fall of established players and their replacement in the public favor by boy actors to fickle public sentiment regarding his father's decease and his uncle's assumption of power. The public is fickle in each case; the loser is easily forgotten. After the scene with Fortinbras's Captain, Hamlet com-

pares himself and Fortinbras, justifiable revenge and unneces-
sary war. After questioning the gravedigger, Hamlet compares
the power of a human in life with the base uses of his body once
he has become dust.

The verbal strategy of inclusion pronounces itself in a second
way, as well, in this brief scene. Hamlet might have said: "How
all occasions do inform against me / And spur my dull revenge!
O, from this time forth, / My thoughts be bloody, or be nothing
worth!" These are the first and last lines of his soliloquy, though,
and what appears in between the frame lines is embellishment.
The effect of the philosophical analysis is a stopping of the
scene, a holding of movement. And there is inclusion within the
inclusion, in, for instance, Hamlet's quartering of a thought.

Word repetition, although it is not a major rhythmic factor in
this scene, serves an interesting function. It separates the exchange between Hamlet and the Captain from the rest of the
scene by patterning it in a special way, but particularly by de-
lineating a progression. The exchange is patterned in other
ways as well. For instance, the questions and answers and the
exchange of philosophies make the unit patterned to begin with.
Word repetition is a rhythmic device woven into the main fabric. The words repeated are quite necessary to the plot. They
are simply "Norway" and "Poland," and through their repeated use, the battle between Norway and Poland is fought
and won by Norway. References to Norway and Poland come increasingly close together. Norway, the aggressor, is always
mentioned first. The word *Norway* always remains intact
whether referring to the country or the man. *Poland* crumbles
conveniently, in poetic terms, to *Pole* and *Polack.*

A good example of word repetition which must be kept subtle
(not emphasized) in production is the use of the word "sir" no
fewer than seven times in this brief exchange. It accounts for
the sense of carefulness, of politeness, and for the low-key quality of the scene. The word is tucked in neatly at various places
in the sentence struture and resolved nicely in the farewells of
Hamlet and the Captain. Overemphasis of the word in a produc-

tion, however, would no doubt give an unfortunate vaudeville or "after you my dear Alphonse" sense to the scene.

No doubt there are other sound repetitions that unite the scene, many of them extremely subtle. It seems likely that the word "go" and its rhymes are functioning early in the scene as a form of sound repetition. At any rate, the repetition of "go" throughout the scene conveys a combination of impending action and momentary calm.

Word repetition functions across scenes as a unifying factor in literature, as word-counters know. In this case, without our being particularly aware of it, we recognize the rightness on some level as Hamlet uses words like "sleep," "feed," "coward," "beast," "reason," in this scene as he has in others. It is aesthetically right, as well as true to the pulse of the piece, that the Captain, like so many others, should begin a speech with a promise of brevity, only to express more than is necessary. There are sense-reminders of earlier scenes, too. The emphasized and memorable "for an eggshell" is an echo of the sense of "for Hecuba." "My thoughts be bloody," is not Hamlet's first attempt to characterize himself as a potentially fiery avenger.

The "eggshell" scene has a number of rhythmic links with other scenes. Some of the rhythms describe the larger sweep of the scene, others the patterning of a specific passage. In the dialogue rhythm of this one scene, there are many echoes of the rest of the play.

So, too, with visual rhythms. Our first image is of a group (Fortinbras and his army) leaving one man (the Captain) alone, if only for a second. Another group picture follows, resolving in Hamlet's solitary occupation of the stage. This is a double use of the dominant visual pattern of the play. Rosencrantz, Guildenstern, and the other guardians assigned to Hamlet constitute his small "army." However, Hamlet is both leader and prisoner. The juxtaposition of Hamlet and his small band of men with Fortinbras and the representatives of his army reminds us that the two young men are fighting an indirect battle and that Fortinbras has greater numbers and more extensive power than does

Hamlet. As Hamlet moves from the direction of the royal dwelling, Fortinbras's envoy moves toward it.

The scene, too, is like the first scene of the play in some ways and serves as a rhythmic repetition of it. Both settings are outdoors and close to the castle, whether realized in scenic detail or not. The first scene is obviously a night scene, and the "eggshell" scene seems like a dark scene or night scene as well. That the scene should be played as a night scene is indicated by Claudius' line of the scene before, "I'll have him hence to-night" (4.3.57), as well as by the quiet and careful tone of the scene's dialogue. The changing of places between Fortinbras and Hamlet is a reminder of the changing of the guard. In the later scene Fortinbras is actually in the vicinity of the castle while he was only imagined to be near at first. There is a good deal of meaning in the automatic crisscross blocking that is demanded by the content of the scene. As is often the case, visual rhythm is expressed in the playing out of visual irony, that is, it is a skimmed down and economized form of progression.

What makes this brief scene function as a rhythmic unit is not only its similarity to and repetition of other scenes in pattern, but in its differences as well. In context it comes after a court scene rather than before, which indicates something of the probability of Hamlet's accomplishing a high tragic revenge. His thoughts have already been bloody, but to no avail. He has already seen the guilt on Claudius' face, but he has not challenged Claudius on the issue. He is being sent away from his prey, and he seems cognizant of the fact that trickery is being employed, but he goes. Fortinbras has obviously grown more powerful and makes Denmark his familiar territory. Yet Hamlet goes. And he goes philosophizing, comparing, gathering evidence still. Since the previous scene ended with the verbalization of Claudius' intent—that England means "the present death of Hamlet"—Hamlet's delay in embarking is again aesthetically justified, just as it will be when he stops by the graveyard on his way back from the ship voyage.

The "eggshell" scene is one of the most political scenes of the play. It can be made more or less so in a production by the degree of military formality both in the stage pictures and in the movement which shows the crisscrossing of the ways of Hamlet and Fortinbras's Captain. A more emotional, psychological interpretation might be pointed up by an actor's playing Hamlet as intentionally delaying, asking questions beyond his desire for answers. Interpretation is somewhat dependent upon which of several existing rhythmic patterns is emphasized.

Rhythm and Mathematics: Speculations

Raymond Bayer says that all art has an unconscious numerical perfection. The working definition in the introduction relates pattern and mathematics: the pattern or mathematics of a play in motion. Examples of the previous chapters have depended most insistently upon the word *irony* to describe the end result of a rhythmic progression. To what extent are all patterns ironic? To what extent are all patterns "mathematical"?

Suppose we are watching a man pacing. He takes ten steps to the left, ten to the right, ten to the left, and ten to the right again. Assuming for the moment that his steps could be equal, which they could not, what we see at any rate is that he ends where he began. Might we say that it is ironic that movement ends in nothing, that the man is back at the beginning? If L stands for leftward movement, his pace might be translated "mathematically" as $+10L - 10L + 10L - 10L = 0L$. Mathematics can generally be reduced to the study of equations: if we attempt to compute the man's pace differently, counting up the total amount of movement, in this case steps (S), regardless of direction or final destination, we get $10S + 10S + 10S + 10S = 40S$. If both equations are correct and we *leap* categories or processes, we get $40S = 0L$, or forty steps equals no movement toward the left. We have certainly stepped out of the realm of legitimate mathematics. Have we stepped into the realm of "artistic mathematics" at all? All irony is the product of some sort

177

of balance or equation of parts. So are paradoxes, but then, paradox is ironic. We have come nowhere near plucking the heart out of art's mystery, because equations in art only point to something immeasurable. For instance, How much internal movement—emotion or thought—has the pace produced in our pacing man? That we cannot measure. Nor can we measure with any exactness his effect on us. We can note that certain changes make the pace comic, or fascinating, or depressing: increasing speed might make it comic; increasing amount of breakup or syncopation might make it fascinating; decreasing speed might make it depressing. Why, in these cases, would increasing speed seem to make us conscious of the physical and spark our laughter, of syncopation remind us of something mental and seem to spark our watchfulness, of decreasing speed seem to convey emotions at work and move us to emotion? We might make some guesses. Does increasing speed "catch us up" and diminish the importance of the pattern? Do we get the feeling that the man does not mind getting back to zero? Does syncopation make us wonder about the infinite number of possibilities within a pattern? Does it make us wonder whether those minor patterns matter since the major pattern will predominate after all? Does decreasing speed give us all the time we need to be aware of pattern, to confirm its existence, so that we watch what seems like resistance to the pattern coupled with depressing inevitability? If we translate speed into closeness of recurrence, do we have anything we can apply to models of comedy, ironic drama, and tragedy? If the pattern of a play is its pattern of ironies, do we have different rhythms of irony in the three somewhat arbitrary classifications which we have become so comfortable with in our need for convenience and order?

If so, how do we explain what seems like a Bergsonian snowball effect in *Oedipus Rex*? If so, why are we not laughing? It may be because our emotions are engaged, as Bergson says. But does the pattern really spend itself so fast in *Oedipus*? If we consider that a first reader of the play knows very early on, and the first audiences knew beforehand, what the answer to the play is (its pattern or irony or equation, if you will), the play takes a relatively long journey to the truth. If we consider that Oedipus is faced with the answer fairly early on in the play, after his interview with Teiresias, there is still a very long period of resistance and a relatively slow putting together of all the parts of the puzzle. The irony is stretched out. Even though the last interview or investigation—the scene with the herdsman— "feels too fast," it is only too fast for the destination. One does not rush to destruction when one can help it. There is an incredible amount of resistance in the final interview scene. The herdsman, of course, continually stalls. But Oedipus does too. He asks all the details, all the little questions, before he gets to the big question. Who would blame him? It would seem rather silly if he asked immediately "Did you take a baby from Laius' house and give it to this man? Is there any chance that I was that child?" These are the kinds of questions and assumptions that tumble out very quickly in the last act of *The Importance of Being Earnest*.

A good example of how a pattern or irony which is not stretched out (and to be fair, not given qualifying detail, i.e., what makes each case different as well as similar) is Bert States's "A Postscript to *Hamlet*." The postscript, which follows, is an introduction to the subject of irony:

> *A tavern in Elsinore. Later that same day.*
> 1 CIT. How came Prince Hamlet by his death?
> 2 CIT. Why, by young Laertes' hand, in revenge for his father's murther.
> 1 CIT. Then—how came Laertes by *his* death?
> 2 CIT. Prince Hamlet slew him, even while avenging *his* father's murther.
> 1 CIT. Go to, go to . . .
> 2 CIT. 'Tis true. And now Fortinbras is crown'd king—
> 1 CIT. Fortinbras next! How comes he into't?
> 2 CIT. Leave off and drink thy ale.[1]

Plot summaries and Tom Stoppard's *Rosencrantz and Guildenstern Are Dead* accomplish the same end by crowding together incidents, reversals, coincidences.

Can rhythm or mathematics in motion be approached by concentration on the ironic poles of a particular play—in what subpatterns they are juxtaposed, with what speed they are juxtaposed? Where is the irony situated in any particular play? Is only the audience aware of the pattern? Are the characters partly aware? Are the characters totally aware? I would venture to say that in most plays all three positions occur at some point or another. So perhaps a better way to phrase the question is, Where is the bulk of ironic recognition—on stage? shared between stage and audience? in the audience?

How complex are the equations? How many missing parts or x's or mysteries exist in the final equation? How has the final equation been arrived at? Through addition, subtraction, multiplication, division, squaring, cubing?

Does our system of balances create any set of expectations? Put a man on a staircase. Suppose he descends seven, ascends six, descends seven, ascends six, descends seven, ascends six, descends—? We not only expect the final seven, but we also do not expect the pattern to end with an ascent to six. It is the wrong direction; it does not balance. We have come to expect that all movement ends one step lower. This pattern might describe what happens to Oedipus and how we *feel* it happening. But there are more ways than one to fall from a height, and playwrights have an infinite number of ways of balancing the falls of their protagonists. Sophocles seems to start Oedipus at the top of a flight of stairs in a tragic world, an automatic signal that he will end at the bottom. Then he brings the protagonist down the steps and sends him up again at fairly regular intervals so that both Oedipus and the spectator get used to the idea of Oedipus at the bottom. This is a gross oversimplification, of course, but it is useful for describing the constant reversals Oedipus experiences and the effect of those reversals. Ibsen's Solness does not really get used to the bottom step via peripety. Ibsen places Solness on a high step, tells us he is afraid of falling, and then allows him to try and avoid the bottom step by climbing higher and higher to make more distance between himself and the bottom. This is as sure a signal as any that he will fall. We are prepared for it by his climbing. And he makes the mistake of all bad climbers, both literally and figuratively. He looks down. Solness' fall is balanced, just as Oedipus' fall is. Oedipus, however, having been close to the bottom, survives his fall, to an extent. Without his eyes or his Thebes there is still a part of him left to contemplate the universal order of things, should he want to. Solness, the voices of the crowd tell us at the end of the play, is fully destroyed. "The head is all crushed.— He fell right into the quarry" (p. 286).

A play need not be stripped of its flesh to prove that all parts of that flesh are joined to the skeleton in some particular and unique way so that the movement of the whole is also unique. It is probably impossible to isolate all the rhythms that make up the major rhythm of a work. Rhythm may be the reason we sense there is something wonderfully full of life and even "life-like" in a work of art.

In *The Lives of a Cell,* a book about the oneness of all life, Lewis Thomas compares words to living creatures. He describes very convincingly how much life they do contain. The phrase "living languages" is not simply an abstract metaphor. To Dr. Thomas, "words are the cells of language, moving the great body, on legs." The comparison is fascinating. "Language grows and evolves, leaving fossils behind. The individual words are like different species of animals. Mutations occur. Words fuse, and then mate. Hybrid words and wild varieties of compound words are the progeny."[2]

If the behavior of words has something akin to the behavior of living creatures, then perhaps both sing or make music in the same ways. Thomas's essay, "The Music of *This* Sphere," keeps reminding me that the biologists' discoveries about the music of the universe parallels the critics' discoveries about the behavior of words in a play. "Leeches have been heard to tap rhythmically on leaves, engaging the attention of other leeches, which tap back, in synchrony. Even earthworms make sounds, faint staccato notes in regular clusters. Toads sing to each other, and their friends sing back in antiphony."[3] Drama is the patterning of words, events, acts, ideas, characters in such a way that they are answers to other words, events, acts, ideas, and characters and in such a way that they also require answers. The first inspiration for this process Suzanne Langer calls Destiny; the process itself Aristotle described in terms of beginning, middle, and end. The arrangement, as it moves and as it moves us, is rhythm.

Notes   /   Index

Notes

Quotations from the plays of Beckett, Chekhov, Ibsen, and Shakespeare are cited in the text. They are from the following sources:

Beckett, Samuel. *Waiting for Godot*. New York: Grove Press, 1961.
Chekhov, Anton. *Four Great Plays*. Trans. Constance Garnett. New York: Grosset & Dunlap, 1968.
Ibsen, Henrik. *Ghosts*. Trans. William Archer. In *A Treasury of the Theatre*. Ed. John Gassner. 2 vols. New York: Holt, Rinehart and Winston, 1961.
_____. *Hedda Gabler, The Master Builder, The Wild Duck*. In *Four Major Plays*. Trans. William Archer. New York: Airmont, 1966.
Shakespeare, William. *The Complete Works*. Ed. Charles Jasper Sisson. New York: Harper and Brothers, 1953.

Chapter 1. Introduction

1. Richard Boleslavsky, *Acting: The First Six Lessons* (New York: Theatre Arts Books, 1963), p. 112.

2. Ibid.

3. See Constantin Stanislavsky, *Building a Character*, trans. Elizabeth Reynolds Hapgood (New York: Theatre Arts Books, 1964), pp. 177–78. Tortsov, who of course represents Stanislavsky, reads the following definition to a class of actors: "Rhythm is the quantitative relationship of units—of movement, of sound—to the unit lengths agreed upon in a given tempo and measure. A measure is a recurrent (or presumably recurrent) group of beats of equal lengths, agreed upon as a unit, and marked by the stress of one of the beats." Tortsov, after reading the definition, throws aside the paper on which it is written, insisting that rhythm is really far more than the scientific definition he has just read. And it is. Yet in Alexander Dean, *Fundamentals of Play Directing*, rev. ed. by Lawrence Carra (New York: Holt, Rinehart and Winston, 1965), p. 234, we find another

definition for theatre based on musical beats and accents: "Rhythm is an experience we receive when a sequence of impressions, auditory or visual, has been ordered into a recurrence of accented groups."

4. Raymond Bayer, "The Essence of Rhythm," in *Reflections on Art*, ed. Suzanne K. Langer (New York: Oxford University Press, 1965), pp. 187–91.

5. Roger Sessions, *The Musical Experience of Composer, Performer, Listener* (New York: Atheneum, 1967), pp. 11–12.

6. Bayer, "Essence of Rhythm," pp. 196, 193, 201.

7. Kenneth Burke, *Counter-Statement*, 2nd ed. (Los Altos, Cal.: Hermes Publications, 1953), pp. 36–37.

8. Suzanne K. Langer, *Feeling and Form* (New York: Charles Scribner's Sons, 1953), pp. 126–27.

9. Ibid., p. 128.

10. Burke, *Counter-Statement*, p. 34.

11. Ibid., p. 31.

12. Bert O. States, *Irony and Drama* (Ithaca, N.Y.: Cornell University Press, 1971), pp. 14, 23.

13. Kenneth Burke, *The Philosophy of Literary Form: Studies in Symbolic Action*, rev. ed., abridged by the author (New York: Random House, 1957), pp. 63–65.

14. Burke, *Counter-Statement*, pp. 33–39.

15. States, *Irony*, p. 116.

16. Langer, *Feeling and Form*, p. 356.

17. Luigi Pirandello, "Preface to *Six Characters in Search of an Author*," in *Naked Masks*, ed. and trans. Eric Bentley (New York: E. P. Dutton, 1952), p. 368.

18. Langer, *Feeling and Form*, p. 322.

Chapter 2. The Open Scene: Meanings Through Rhythm

1. This open scene was composed by the author. For a discussion of the use of this and other similar dialogues, see Wandalie Henshaw, "The 'Open Scene' as a Directing Exercise," *Educational Theatre Journal* 21 (Oct. 1969), 275–84.

2. Kenneth Burke, *Counter-Statement*, 2nd ed. (Los Altos, Cal.: Hermes Publications, 1953), pp. 133–34.

3. Ibid., p. 136.

4. Northrop Frye, *Anatomy of Criticism: Four Essays* (Princeton, N.J.: Princeton University Press, 1957), p. 271.

Chapter 3. Repetition of Sounds, Words, and Phrases

1. Plays that are discussed and quoted frequently will be cited in the text. The editions I have used are listed at the beginning of the Notes.

2. See the translation by Una Ellis-Fermor in *"Hedda Gabler" and Other Plays* (Harmondsworth, Middlesex, England: Penguin Books, 1973), p. 156, and

the translation by R. Farquharson Sharp in *Four Great Plays by Henrik Ibsen* (New York: Bantam, 1971), p. 230.

3. Harold Pinter, *A Slight Ache,* in *Three Plays* (New York: Grove Press, 1962), p. 9. All later quotations from *A Slight Ache* in the text are from this edition.

4. William L. Sharp, *Language in Drama* (Scranton, Pa.: Chandler, 1970), p. 120.

5. *Sunday Times* (London), Mar. 4, 1962, cited in ibid., p. 119.

6. Henri Bergson, "Laughter," in *Comedy* (Garden City, N.Y.: Doubleday, 1956), p. 84.

7. Northrop Frye, *Anatomy of Criticism: Four Essays* (Princeton, N.J.: Princeton University Press, 1957), p. 278.

8. Edward Albee, *A Delicate Balance* (New York: Pocket Books, 1970), pp. 13-15.

9. (New York: Charles Scribner's Sons, 1953), p. 281.

10. Martin Esslin, *The Theatre of the Absurd* (Garden City, N.Y.: Doubleday, 1961), p. 296.

11. Ibid., p. 241.

12. Andrew Welsh, "Melos and Opsis" (Ph.D. diss., University of Pittsburgh, 1970), pp. 150, 155, 157. See also his recently published book, *Roots of Lyric* (Princeton, N.J.: Princeton University Press, 1978).

13. Esslin, *Theatre of the Absurd,* pp. 25-26.

14. Günther Müller, "Morphological Poetics," in *Reflections on Art,* ed. Suzanne K. Langer (New York: Oxford University Press, 1965), p. 205.

15. In *The Philosophy of Literary Form: Studies in Symbolic Action,* rev. ed., abridged by the author (New York: Random House, 1957), pp. 296-304.

16. Robert Brustein, *The Theatre of Revolt* (Boston: Little, Brown, 1964), p. 167.

17. *The Elements of Drama* (Cambridge: Cambridge University Press, 1967), pp. 211-12.

18. Frye, *Anatomy of Criticism,* p. 285.

19. Bert O. States, *Irony and Drama* (Ithaca, N.Y.: Cornell University Press, 1971), p. 108.

Chapter 4. Alternation of Speaker and Length of Speech

1. Richard Boleslavsky, *Acting: The First Six Lessons* (New York: Theatre Arts Books, 1963), p. 119.

2. Kenneth Burke, *Counter-Statement,* 2nd ed. (Los Altos, Cal.: Hermes Publications, 1953), pp. 126-27.

3. Friedrich von Schiller, "On the Use of the Chorus in Tragedy," trans. A. Lodge, in *Theatre and Drama in the Making,* ed. John Gassner and Ralph G. Allen, 2 vols. (Boston: Houghton Mifflin, 1964), 1: 71.

4. Ibid., pp. 64–65.

5. Richmond Lattimore, "Introduction," *Aeschylus I: Oresteia,* trans. Richmond Lattimore (Chicago: University of Chicago Press, 1966), 1:25.

6. Sophocles, *Oedipus the King,* trans. David Grene, in *An Anthology of Greek Drama,*, ed. Charles Alexander Robinson, Jr. (New York: Holt, Rinehart and Winston, 1962), pp. 62–68.

7. Bert O. States, "The Word-Pictures in *Hamlet,*" *Hudson Review* 26 (Autumn 1973), 513.

8. Ibid.

9. Gisèle Brelet, "Music and Silence," in *Reflections on Art,* ed. Suzanne K. Langer (New York: Oxford University Press, 1965) p. 105.

10. Ibid., p. 106.

Chapter 5. Repetition of Verbal Strategy

1. John C. Condon, Jr., *Semantics and Communication* (New York: Macmillan, 1966), p. 63.

2. Noel Coward, *Hay Fever* (New York: Samuel French, 1954), p. 14. Hereafter cited in the text.

3. *Hudson Review* 26 (Autumn 1973), 512–13.

4. Ibid., p. 520.

Chapter 6. Patterning of Attitude

1. John C. Condon, Jr., *Semantics and Communication* (New York: Macmillan, 1966), p. 90.

Chapter 7. Style

1. Northrop Frye, *Anatomy of Criticism: Four Essays* (Princeton, N.J.: Princeton University Press, 1957), p. 268.

2. Ibid.

3. Ibid., p. 269.

4. Kenneth Burke, *Counter-Statement,* 2nd ed. (Los Altos, Cal.: Hermes Publications, 1953), p. 124.

5. August Strindberg, *The Father,* trans. Edith and Warner Oland, in *A Treasury of the Theatre,* ed. John Gassner, 2 vols. (New York: Holt, Rinehart and Winston, 1961), 2:91.

6. Burke, *Counter-Statement,* pp. 124–25.

7. Maxim Gorki, *The Lower Depths,* trans. Jenny Covan, in Gassner, *Treasury,* 2:242.

8. Frye, *Anatomy of Criticism,* p. 269.

9. Oscar Wilde, *The Importance of Being Earnest,* in *Eight Great Comedies,*

ed. Sylvan Barnet, Morton Berman, and William Burto (New York: New American Library, 1964), p. 290. Hereafter cited in the text.

10. Frye, *Anatomy of Criticism*, p. 269.

11. Sean O'Casey, *The Plough and the Stars*, in Gassner, *Treasury*, 2:636.

12. Frye, *Anatomy of Criticism*, p. 268.

13. Burke, *Counter-Statement*, p. 1.

14. David Gillès, *Chekhov: Observer Without Illusion*, trans. Charles Lam Markmann (New York: Funk and Wagnalls, 1968), p. 348.

Chapter 8. The Single Scene

1. Richard Boleslavsky, *Acting: The First Six Lessons* (New York: Theatre Arts Books, 1963), p. 114.

2. Adolph Appia, *The Work of Living Art*, trans. H. D. Albright (Coral Gables, Florida: University of Miami Press, 1960), pp. 113–15.

3. In *Theatre and Drama in the Making*, ed. John Gassner and Ralph G. Allen, 2 vols. (Boston: Houghton Mifflin, 1964), 2:568–69.

4. August Strindberg, *The Father*, trans. Edith and Warner Oland, in *A Treasury of the Theatre*, ed. John Gassner, 2 vols. (New York: Holt, Rinehart and Winston, 1961), 2:78, 85, 90.

5. Francis Fergusson, "The Tragic Rhythm in a Small Figure," in *Ibsen: A Collection of Critical Essays*, ed. Rolf Fjelde (Englewood Cliffs, N.J.: Prentice-Hall, 1965), p. 112.

6. Ibid., p. 118.

7. Ralph G. Allen, "*Ghosts*," a lecture presented at the University of Pittsburgh, Pittsburgh, Pa., 1963.

8. Samuel Beckett, *Happy Days* (New York: Grove Press, 1961), p. 13. Hereafter cited in the text.

Chapter 9. The Polyscenic Stage

1. *Early English Stages: 1300–1600*, 2 vols. (New York: Columbia University Press, 1959), 1:89.

2. Martial Rose, ed., "Introduction," *The Wakefield Mystery Plays* (Garden City, N.Y.: Doubleday, 1963), p. 34.

3. Ibid., p. 36.

4. Ibid.

Chapter 10. The Panoramic Stage

1. The "inner stage" theory, now discounted, presupposed a separate acting area in the tiring house. Just where these scenes *were* played is still a subject of controversy.

2. Nevill Coghill, *Shakespeare's Professional Skills* (Cambridge: Cambridge University Press, 1964), pp. 64–65.

3. Harley Granville-Barker, "Shakespeare's Dramatic Art," in *A Companion to Shakespeare Studies,* ed. Harley Granville-Barker and G. B. Harrison (New York: Macmillan, 1934), p. 71.

4. Ibid., p. 62.

5. John L. Styan, *Shakespeare's Stagecraft* (Cambridge: Cambridge University Press, 1967), pp. 121–22.

6. Bertolt Brecht, *Mother Courage and Her Children,* trans. Eric Bentley (New York: Grove Press, 1966), p. 82.

Chapter 11. The Limited Scenic Progression

1. Robert Brustein, *The Theatre of Revolt* (Boston: Little, Brown, 1964), pp. 155–79.

2. George Bernard Shaw, *Arms and the Man,* in *Eight Great Comedies,* ed. Sylvan Barnet, Morton Berman, and William Burto (New York: New American Library, 1964), p. 392. Hereafter cited in the text.

Chapter 12. Symbolic Gesture

1. George Bernard Shaw, *Arms and the Man,* in *Eight Great Comedies,* ed. Sylvan Barnet, Morton Berman, and William Burto (New York: New American Library, 1964), pp. 392–93. Hereafter cited in the text.

2. Caroline W. Mayerson, "Thematic Symbols in *Hedda Gabler,*" in *Ibsen: A Collection of Critical Essays,* ed. Rolf Fjelde (Englewood Cliffs, N.J.: Prentice-Hall, 1965), pp. 136–37.

3. Bert O. States, *Irony and Drama* (Ithaca, N.Y.: Cornell University Press, 1971), p. 153.

4. Euripides, *Hippolytus,* trans. Arthur S. Way, in *An Anthology of Greek Drama* (New York: Holt, Rinehart and Winston, 1962), p. 225.

5. *Analogy* is Francis Fergusson's word for a particular kind of rhythmic patterning in drama. He has shown us a number of progressions in *Hamlet*— public and private scenes, ritual and improvisational scenes—as well as pointing to action by *analogy.* He specifically pinpoints the "indirectness" of approach of all characters in *Hamlet* as they attempt to find and destroy the evil or disease of Denmark, which to each of them is something different. See "*Hamlet, Prince of Denmark:* The Analogy of Action," *The Idea of a Theatre* (Princeton, N.J.: Princeton University Press, 1972), pp. 98–142.

Chapter 14. Rhythm and Mathematics: Speculations

1. Bert O. States, *Irony and Drama* (Ithaca, N.Y.: Cornell University Press, 1971), p. 2.

2. Lewis Thomas, *The Lives of a Cell* (New York: Viking Press, 1974), p. 135.

3. Ibid., p. 22.

Index